QUESTIONS & ANSWERS:
Criminal Law

Multiple Choice and Short Answer
Questions and Answers

By

Emily Marcus Levine, Esquire
and

Paul Marcus
Haynes Professor of Law
College of William and Mary

LexisNexis™

ISBN#: 0820556629

Editorial Offices
744 Broad Street, Newark, NJ 07102 (973) 820-2000
201 Mission St., San Francisco, CA 94105-1831 (415) 908-3200
701 East Water Street, Charlottesville, VA 22902-7587 (804) 972-7600
www.lexis.com

(Pub.3176)

ABOUT THE AUTHORS

Emily Marcus Levine graduated from the University of Virginia Law School in 1998 and clerked for the United States District Court for the Eastern District of Virginia in 1999. She is currently an attorney with the Office of the General Counsel of the United States Department of Health and Human Services, where she specializes in legal issues relating to organ and bone marrow transplantation and vaccine injury compensation.

Paul Marcus is the Haynes Professor of Law at the College of William and Mary, Williamsburg, Virginia. He has written casebooks and treatises in both criminal law and criminal procedure, and has lectured on these topics throughout the United States and in many foreign nations as well. He is the former Law Dean at the University of Arizona, and Interim Law Dean at William and Mary.

PREFACE

The study of criminal law in the first year of law school (for most students) involves a rich overview of the United States criminal justice system, explores questions as to why, whom and how we punish, and requires us to face squarely the relationship of the individual to the state. The issues considered in the class are some of the most disturbing and important found throughout the law school curriculum: What are the limits on the ability of the state to sanction behavior? What is appropriate punishment for crimes? What evidence is sufficient to demonstrate a culpable state of mind? Should we have a felony murder rule? Does it make sense to establish degrees of murder? The crime of conspiracy casts a wide net of criminal responsibility, is the crime justified? In relieving defendants of responsibility, have we as a society grown to rely too heavily on defenses such as self-defense, necessity, entrapment and insanity?

The key to learning criminal law is to ask, and then answer, several questions about each problem. These include:

(1) What crime is charged-the answer is not always self evident, as the differences between crimes such as second degree murder and involuntary manslaughter, for instance, can be subtle.

(2) Is the crime within the permissible scope of legislative action-are there some activities which simply cannot be prohibited by the state?

(3) What are the elements of the crime-laying out the elements of *actus reus, mens rea* and causation is not difficult, defining particular elements (such as the act requirement for the attempt offense) can be very tough.

(4) What is the standard of review to determine if the case can proceed-has the government offered sufficient evidence such that a reasonable person could find all the elements of the crime, beyond a reasonable doubt?

(5) What evidence has the government brought forth to prove its case-often the prosecution will base its theory heavily, if not entirely, on circumstantial evidence while defense counsel will argue that such evidence is not persuasive.

(6) Can the defendant rebut the government's case by offering evidence of an affirmative defense-some of the defenses play a large role in the determination of criminal responsibility.

In answering these questions, we encourage you to do so as carefully as you can, whether in responding with short answers or in analyzing the multiple choices given. Your inclination might be to look at the question, think briefly about the answer, and then read the one that we have prepared. Going through the question thoroughly, however, will prove far more beneficial to you in developing your understanding of the underlying issues presented in the questions.

While the questions and answers you will read in this book contain a considerable amount of information, our purpose here is not to teach a short course in criminal law. Rather, we hope these materials will test your knowledge of the key principles in the subject and how they ought to be viewed as a whole. The book is designed as a supplement to the course casebook you will be assigned by your criminal law professor. You will find questions and answers in seven principal subject areas that correspond to the main topics most teachers cover in the introductory criminal law course: *Limits on the Criminal Sanction, Elements of the Offense, Parties to Crimes, Inchoate Offenses, Crimes, Causation,* and *Defenses.* This book is organized in much the same way as many of the more popular criminal law casebooks. Still, even if your professor covers the material in a different order the book should be helpful to you.

The problems in this book are not keyed to any one body of criminal law such as Federal law, the Model Penal Code or any one or more particular states. Instead, the problems are based on the majority principles, with notations as to significant minority views or developing modern trends. This approach is much the same as used by those who have developed the Multistate Bar Examination.

We wish you good luck with your study of the fascinating and important matters you will see in criminal law.

Paul Marcus
Williamsburg, VA

Emily Marcus Levine
Washington, D.C
April, 2003

TABLE OF CONTENTS

QUESTIONS

Responding to merchant complaints about addicts congregating by fancy stores, the legislature passed a new law making it a crime "to be addicted to the use of illegal narcotics." Walking on the public street, Charlie was seen by a police officer to be moving unsteadily. The officer approached Charlie and asked him, "Are you OK?" Charlie responded, "None of your business. I just shot up, and it takes me a while to come back down." Charlie was then arrested and charged with violating the new law.

1.   Can he be successfully prosecuted?

   (A)   Yes, the officer's observation would clearly be sufficient evidence to convict Charlie.

   (B)   Yes, the officer's observation, coupled with Charlie's statement, would be sufficient evidence to convict.

   (C)   No, the conviction would violate Charlie's constitutional rights.

   (D)   No, Charlie's statement could not be used against him.

2.   Could Charlie be successfully prosecuted for the crime of being under the influence of narcotics while in public?

ANSWER:

3.   Does the result above change if Charlie offered convincing evidence both that he was addicted to narcotics and that he was a homeless person who was on the street because he had no other alternative?

   (A)   Yes, because Charlie is an addict and homeless, punishing him for this crime when he has nowhere else to go would violate the Constitution.

   (B)   Yes, because Charlie is an addict and his disease compels him to take drugs, it would be cruel and unusual punishment to convict him for his status, rather than for a voluntary action that he undertook.

   (C)   No, because the law against being under the influence in public has been published in the state code, all citizens are presumed to know that this conduct is illegal.

   (D)   No. Although Charlie is an addict, he does not lack free will. Because he could choose not to take drugs or not to do so in a public place, convicting him of being under the influence in public would not be prohibited.

A police officer pulled over Jo and arrested her for "reckless driving," based on the observation of her erratic lane changing. Jo's lawyer asserts that the statute should be declared vague for voidness, insofar as the state legislature never defined what actions were intended to be prohibited in the law.

    4.   Can Jo nonetheless be convicted?

ANSWER:

[A] The Act

[1] Failure to Act

Erin passed an accident on her way home from work. A car had run off the road and hit a tree, and the driver was unconscious and seriously injured. In a hurry to get home, Erin decided to continue on her way, certain that someone else would stop and offer assistance. The following day, the driver of the car died.

5. If the police learn that Erin drove by the accident, but did not intervene, can she be held criminally liable?

   (A) Yes, because the victim was in grave danger, Erin owed a duty to help him.

   (B) Yes, because Erin may have been the only person who could have helped the victim.

   (C) No, because only medical professionals could be required to help the driver.

   (D) No, because generally there is no duty for anyone to assist others.

6. Would the result change if Erin were a highway patrol officer who passed the accident, and decided not to stop or phone in a report because her shift was to end soon, and she did not want to be delayed?

ANSWER:

Troy was involved in a car accident in which the driver of the other car was seriously injured. Fearful that he would be unfairly blamed for the collision, Troy drove away without rendering aid or reporting the accident.

7. Can Troy be successfully prosecuted for his conduct *after* the accident?

   (A) Yes, being in the accident created a greater moral obligation on Troy's part.

   (B) Yes, most states require immediate assistance and/or reporting after an accident.

   (C) No, there is no duty generally to assist others.

   (D) No, there is no duty to assist others unless Troy had been at fault in causing the collision.

Matthew and his ex-wife had been divorced for two years. He and ex-his wife had joint custody of their young children and the children often spent weekends away with her. On several occasions, after they returned to his home, Matthew noticed burn marks on his daughter's arm. When he asked his daughter about this, she said that sometimes she was a bad girl and her mother had to punish her. Matthew knew that his ex-wife had been violent with the children in the past. However, he was scared of starting another custody battle with his ex-wife because she had threatened to "dig up some dirt" on him. Matthew did not bring up the issue with his ex-wife or with anyone else.

8.   Can Matthew be held criminally liable for the harm to the child?

   (A)   Yes; because of his special relationship with his children, Matthew's failure to act makes him responsible for their abuse.

   (B)   Yes, because he chose to become involved when he asked his daughter about her injuries.

   (C)   No, because Matthew had no affirmative duty to act and he had no direct role in inflicting the abuse.

   (D)   No. Matthew's ex-wife is the truly culpable party in this situation.

Marianna harbored a deep hatred of her sister Katherine. After years of growing resentment, Marianna was consumed with jealousy of her more successful, intelligent, and attractive sister. She began to craft an elaborate plan to kill her sister. However, before she took any steps to commit the murder, her plot was discovered.

9.   Can Marianna be held criminally liable for her scheme?

ANSWER:

[2] The Voluntary Act

Betty drove two of her friends home from work. On the drive, she lost control of the car and slammed into a big tree. Both friends were killed. Apparently, while driving, Betty lost consciousness and just ran off the road. A later medical examination indicates that Betty had an undiagnosed brain disorder in the portion of her brain that regulated consciousness, and this disorder very likely caused her to become unconscious while driving that night.

10.   Can Betty be held criminally responsible for the deaths of her friends?

   (A)   No, because the law only punishes people for voluntary acts and Betty did not act voluntarily.

   (B)   No, because Betty was only offering assistance in driving the others, and the law does not punish good Samaritans.

   (C)   Yes, because Betty could still be convicted even without a voluntary act.

   (D)   Yes, because Betty committed a voluntary act when she agreed to drive passengers.

11. Would the result change if Betty knew of her medical problem, but decided to drive anyway because it was such a short ride?

ANSWER:

Two police officers arrived at a downtown apartment house in response to complaints from neighbors about a noisy party. Morgan answered the door, clearly inebriated. The officers told him to step outside to the sidewalk so that they could talk to him, insinuating that he would get into trouble if he did not do as told. Morgan went outside to speak with the officers. When Morgan reached the sidewalk, the officers arrested him for being drunk in public.

12. Can Morgan be convicted?

(A) Yes, because the statute does not require a voluntary act.

(B) Yes, because Morgan committed the voluntary act when he drank alcohol.

(C) No, because a voluntary act requirement will be implied, and Morgan did not act in such a manner as to violate the statute.

(D) No, because even if a voluntary act requirement is implied, Morgan did not violate the statute.

[B] The Mental State

For two years, Rick had been leaving his two young daughters in the care of his live-in girlfriend, Tamika. Though Tamika had a nasty temper, Rick loved her. The situation worked out well for him because he worked nights and the girls could remain at home with Tamika. One morning when he returned home from work, his oldest daughter was on the living room floor, crying, in obvious pain. Tamika claimed nothing odd had occurred the previous night, but after the girl's condition did not improve throughout the day, Rick grew concerned that she was very sick and brought her to the hospital. The emergency room doctor determined that the girl had been beaten in the abdomen and severely injured. Tamika fled and was never found. Rick was later charged with felony child abuse, for "knowingly subjecting a child to significant injury or neglect."

13. If the state demonstrates that Rick's younger child had been treated for a similar injury while staying with Tamika several months before this incident, could Rick be convicted on this charge?

(A) No, because Rick had no way to know his girlfriend might be abusing his daughter.

(B) No, because it is unfair to hold Rick responsible for the actions of his girlfriend.

(C) Yes, because the previous incident combined with his awareness of Tamika's temper means that Rick knew his girlfriend could be violent and posed a serious risk to his daughters.

    (D) No, because the evidence could not establish that Rick had knowledge of a serious risk.

Frieda was pulled over for speeding in her car. While he was issuing her a ticket, the officer noticed an open gas can on the floor of her car. In addition to the speeding ticket, he also charged her with unsafe handling of explosives, which makes it a criminal action to "knowingly transport highly flammable or toxic materials in an unsafe manner." Frieda contends that although she did know the open gas can was in her car, she did not know that this was a crime.

    14.   Can she establish a viable defense to the charge?

ANSWER:

Adam met up with several friends after work on Friday evening and had dinner. Over the course of a couple of hours, they enjoyed a decent meal, split a few bottles of wine, and discussed the events of the previous week. Adam departed early and headed home, only to be pulled over by a highway patrolman. The officer suspected that Adam was drunk, conducted a field sobriety test, and Adam's blood alcohol level was above the legal limit. The officer arrested him for driving while intoxicated. Adam, shocked that he would be considered drunk after only a few glasses of wine, considered this charge most unfair.

    15.   Which of the following arguments might successfully be put forth in his defense?

    (A) He did not know that he was intoxicated.

    (B) He did not intend to drive while intoxicated.

    (C) Any reasonable person would have acted in the same manner, considering the circumstances.

    (D) None of the above.

Suppose Adam was in an accident in the above example. He was driving home and accidentally hit a young girl crossing the street at an intersection. The girl was very badly injured, but she survived.

    16.   What additional crime might Adam be found guilty of due to the accident?

    (A) Attempted murder.

    (B) Reckless endangerment.

    (C) Manslaughter.

    (D) Negligent homicide.

While drinking in a bar, Mauricio got angry at another patron's insults and tried to punch him. The insulting guy ducked, though, and Mauricio accidentally punched a woman standing behind him, breaking her nose. Mauricio is charged with battery, which requires an "intentional act to injure another through physical contact."

17. Will he be found guilty?

(A) Yes, because even if Mauricio did not intend to hit the person injured, he did intend to hit another person.

(B) Yes, because the intent to hit someone is unnecessary.

(C) No, because Mauricio did not intend to hit the person injured.

(D) No, because Mauricio's intent to hit the man who insulted him was justified.

Holly often visited her ailing uncle in prison. She was having a drink one afternoon and told the barkeep at the local pub that on Sundays she visited the penitentiary. The bartender asked if, while she was visiting, she would visit *his* uncle and give him the weather report. Holly thought this was a bit odd, but the bartender assured her that his uncle used to travel a lot and just liked to hear about the weather in cities he knew. The bartender promised to provide her the weather information every week if she would give his uncle the message. The weather reports Holly later conveyed seemed to make the bartender's uncle very happy. Holly was later charged with "knowingly assisting organized crime." The government asserts that the weather reports were actually coded messages about the activities of a local crime syndicate. Holly claimed she did not know anything about any criminal activity, and the prosecution does not challenge her claim.

18. If she truly did not know about the secret nature of the messages, could she be convicted?

(A) Yes, because she knew that she was delivering information, which in fact assisted the syndicate.

(B) Yes, because the knowledge requirement includes an objective evaluation, and a reasonable person would have known that these messages were not innocuous.

(C) No, because Holly did not in fact know that the weather reports were assisting the criminal activity.

(D) No, because Holly should only be held if she intended to assist the syndicate.

Bill drove a large truck as part of his tree removal business. For years, he parked his truck along the driveway in front of his home without any problems. He did this because he never even considered the situation to be risky, even though the overhead power lines fall within a few feet of the top of his truck. While climbing on his truck, a neighborhood child was injured by the overhead power lines.

19. Putting aside any issues of civil liability, can Bill be found guilty under a statute criminalizing "reckless behavior on one's property which results in an injury to others"?

    (A)   Yes, because Bill should have seen the risks inherent in his actions, parking the truck under the power lines.

    (B)   Yes, because his behavior caused a substantial, unjustifiable risk.

    (C)   No, because although his behavior caused an unjustifiable risk, Bill was not aware of the risk.

    (D)   No, because it is not clear that Bill's actions caused the risk to the child.

Victoria got in a heated argument with her boyfriend. Eventually, the boyfriend ran at her with a large chef's knife. Victoria wrestled it away from him, but during the struggle the knife fell and badly cut the boyfriend's foot, resulting in serious injury.

    20.   Putting aside any affirmative defenses, can Victoria be convicted of intentional wounding?

ANSWER:

Trisha went out to a bar with some friends and got extremely drunk. She and her companions shared a cab ride home. When Trisha arrived at her apartment house, she was unable to get in her door because her key kept getting jammed in the lock. As she had done on several previous occasions, she pried open the screen on the outside window and climbed inside. Once she was in the living room, a police officer arrived. Apparently, Trisha had mistakenly broken into her neighbor's apartment. She was arrested for attempted burglary.

    21.   Can Trisha successfully defend by claiming she was just mistaken and thought that she was breaking into her own apartment?

    (A)   Yes, such a mistake of fact can act as a defense.

    (B)   Yes, mistake of fact can be offered to disprove that she had intended a burglary.

    (C)   No, Trisha was mistaken only as to the apartment she entered, not as to her actions.

    (D)   No, because mistake of law is not a defense.

Defendant was charged with attempted murder after he planted a bomb on a commuter train full of people. The bomb was inoperable, as it did not have a necessary component that would allow it to detonate. Although the bomb was harmless, there was much media coverage of its discovery because the train was filled with hundreds of people. The defendant asserts that he knew the bomb would not work and that he wanted merely to show that security measures are lacking in the country's transportation system.

    22.   If he is believed, will this argument allow him to successfully rebut the government's case for attempted murder?

ANSWER:

Jorge owned a manufacturing plant. He realized that it would be much cheaper to dump polluted water from the manufacturing process into the adjacent river rather than pipe the water through an expensive filtering process. He asked his lawyer Delia whether dumping the water into the river would violate any laws. Delia assured him, in an opinion letter, that such action would not violate the law. After dumping the water into the river, Jorge was prosecuted for polluting river water.

23. Will his reliance on Delia's advice defeat the charge?

   (A) Yes, Jorge's reliance was reasonable.

   (B) Yes, he did not realize it was against the law to dump the water into the river.

   (C) No, relying on the advice of a lawyer generally cannot be used against a criminal charge.

   (D) No, the crime is likely a strict liability offense.

24. Would the answer change if Jorge relied on the statement to him made by the head of the State Attorney General's Office on Environmental Control, instead of by his own lawyer?

ANSWER:

Tabitha's boyfriend told her about his plan to rob a bank with a friend. Although Tabitha expressed concerns about the scheme, especially that they might get caught and go to prison, she did not do anything to stop her boyfriend from carrying out his plan. Several days before the robbery was to take place, Tabitha's boyfriend asked her if she would go to the coffee shop next to the bank, sit outside, and alert him if anything untoward happened outside while the robbery was taking place. Tabitha agreed and did so on the day of the robbery. The robbery was interrupted in the progress, and the actors were arrested and charged.

25. Under common law rules, can Tabitha be held responsible as a party to the robbery?

(A) No, she cannot be held liable as a party to the crime because she was not directly involved in the criminal enterprise.

(B) Yes, she can be held liable as a principal in the first degree.

(C) Yes, she can be held liable as a principal in the second degree.

(D) Yes, she can be held responsible as an accessory before the fact.

Assume that in the above example, Tabitha's boyfriend never told her of his plan to rob the bank. Tabitha did not act as a lookout, nor did she know of her boyfriend's desire to commit such a crime. Her boyfriend and a couple of his buddies showed up at Tabitha's apartment after the robbery and asked her if they could all go to her parents' mountain cabin for a week or so. Tabitha was surprised and she asked, "What's the hurry?" Her boyfriend told her that he and his friends had just robbed a bank and they needed to get out of town and lay low for a while. Tabitha laughed at them, assuming that he was joking with her. Tabitha consented and the group went to the cabin for a week. Several months later, Tabitha's boyfriend and his friends were arrested for the robbery.

26. Under the modern approach, can Tabitha be found a party to the robbery? Would the result change if Tabitha knew that her boyfriend robbed two banks in the past?

ANSWER:

Big Jim runs a clandestine gambling operation. One night his neighbor Stan stopped by and placed a few bets. At the end of the night, Stan looked at his winnings and felt strongly that Big Jim cheated him. A few days later, Stan discovered that Big Jim had also suckered his business partner Bill into losing money. Bill told Stan that he wanted to find out where Big Jim lived, so Bill could "rough him up" and "make that jerk sorry for what he did." Because he felt cheated, Stan gave Big Jim's address to Bill. Several days later, Big Jim was assaulted by Bill and brought to the hospital with serious injuries. Bill was picked up by the police and charged with the beating.

27. Can Stan be convicted as a party to the assault under the modern approach?

   (A) No, because Stan did not take any part in the attack.

   (B) No, because merely providing Bill with Big Jim's address was insufficient for Bill to be held criminally liable.

   (C) Yes, because Stan knew of Bill's intentions and assisted him by providing him with information.

   (D) Yes, because Stan hoped that Bill would assault Big Jim.

28. Suppose in the above example that Stan provided Bill with Big Jim's address. However, the following day, Bill attacked Big Jim after running into him in a convenience store. Given that the information Stan provided to Bill was not used when Bill carried out the crime, can Stan still be held liable as a party to the battery under the modern approach?

ANSWER:

Ellen intended to help Jason commit a burglary. Low on cash, she agreed to drive him to the house of his choice in exchange for a cut of the proceeds. Ellen drove and Jason went into the house and returned to the car about thirty minutes later with some goods from the house. Later, Ellen discovered that in addition to stealing a few items from the house, Jason also sexually assaulted a woman who was inside.

29. Can Ellen be held liable as an accomplice in the assault?

   (A) No, because Ellen did not intend for the assault to be committed.

   (B) No, because Ellen did not commit an act in furtherance of the assault.

   (C) Yes, because Ellen intended that a crime be committed.

   (D) Yes, Ellen is liable as a partner in crime even though she did not know all of her partner's intentions.

In the above problem, assume that Jason intended only to burglarize the house and that he did not assault the woman inside. Instead, while Jason was in the process of gathering valuables, the owner of the house surprised Jason and pointed a gun at him. Jason reacted by shooting the owner of the house. The owner died instantly.

30. Will Ellen be liable for the murder of the house's owner?

ANSWER:

Amanda and Lance often had lunch together and discussed their workplace gripes. One afternoon, Lance described how his boss repeatedly berated and humiliated him. Lance said that he would love to make his boss "pay" for the way she treated him. Amanda, sympathetic to her friend's story, agreed, remarking, "it's not like she doesn't deserve it. I heard she treats her husband the same way. She has something coming to her." A few days later, Lance attempted to cut the brake line in his boss's car, hoping that the car would wreck and that his boss would have a serious accident. Lance was arrested for tampering with his boss's car.

31. Did the conversation in the lunchroom provide for criminal liability on Amanda's part?

   (A) Yes, because Amanda intended to encourage Lance to take the action he did.

   (B) Yes, because Amanda encouraged Lance to take such an action.

   (C) No, because the First Amendment protects freedom of speech.

   (D) No, because Amanda did not demonstrate the requisite intent for Lance to commit the crime.

Floyd, Aiden, and Mike formed a plan to kidnap the daughter of a wealthy businesswoman and hold her for ransom. They spent months planning the time and place for the abduction, as well as their intended negotiation strategy with the family and the authorities. On the designated date, the three were to meet at the city park across from the girl's school and kidnap her as she left school for the day. Mike never showed up. Floyd and Aiden proceeded with the plan anyway and took the girl to a remote cabin. Shortly after they arrived at the cabin, Aiden began to grow anxious and started to feel sorry for the girl. Aiden decided to go home and he tried to convince Floyd that holding the girl was a lost cause, reminding him that the girl was always crying. He argued that they would never see any ransom and would soon be apprehended. Floyd did not agree, insisting that any day the money would be wired into the designated bank account and that the two of them would be able to go to Geneva as planned. Aiden left the cabin and returned home, giving up on the plan. After following the story on the news for a few days, Aiden called the police and provided the location of the cabin. The girl was returned home safely.

32. Putting aside conspiracy charges, can Mike be found responsible for the kidnapping, as a party to the crime?

   (A) No, Mike withdrew before the crime was committed.

   (B) No, Mike never involved himself in the crime.

   (C) Yes, Mike never effectively withdrew from the enterprise.

   (D) Yes, once engaged in the enterprise, Mike could not withdraw without any liability.

33. Will Aiden be found responsible?

ANSWER:

Private citizen Salma bribed government official Pierre by giving him first class airplane tickets in exchange for favorable treatment on a construction project. Salma was charged with the giving of the bribe and Pierre was charged with the receiving of the bribe. Pierre, in a January trial, was acquitted of the charge, arguing that he did not realize it was unlawful to take airplane tickets. In August, at a separate trial, Salma was convicted of giving the bribe to Pierre. She argues, on appeal, that because Pierre was acquitted of receiving the bribe, her conviction for giving the bribe to Pierre cannot stand.

34.   Will she win this argument?

ANSWER:

[A] Solicitation

Peter and Wendy were talking at a neighborhood barbeque, and Peter began discussing his marital problems. Wendy commented that Peter would be better off without his wife, and that if his wife were out of the picture, perhaps Wendy and Peter could get together. It appeared that Peter took this comment seriously, mentioning to Wendy later that night some possible methods of eliminating his wife. After several weeks, Peter's behavior grew increasingly odd and he talked about the earlier conversation at the party several times. Wendy grew concerned that he was giving serious consideration to killing his wife. Wendy approached him to tell him she was only joking at the party, but Peter laughed off her concerns. Several days later, Peter attempted to kill his wife.

35. Is Wendy guilty of solicitation?

ANSWER:

Miguel and Steven were two high school students eating lunch in the cafeteria. Their conversation was cut short when Carter, a hulking brute, began taunting a student at the next table about her clothing. Steven said to Miguel, "Somebody ought to give that guy what he deserves." Several days later, Miguel slashed Carter's tires.

36. Is Steven guilty of the crime of solicitation?

(A) Yes, because Steven was the creative force behind the crime.

(B) Yes, because Steven encouraged Mike to commit the crime.

(C) No, because Miguel was the only one to commit an affirmative act toward the crime.

(D) No, because Steven did not intend for Miguel to slash Carter's tires.

On several occasions, Samantha heard the new waiter at the restaurant where she worked talk about "doing drugs." She approached him and asked if he knew where she could obtain some marijuana. He responded that he was not sure, but he could ask around. Samantha thanked him and gave him some cash, saying, "This should cover the cost if you happen to locate any for me. If you can't find any, just give me the cash back. I'm sure you're good for it." However, the new waiter was actually a police officer conducting an undercover investigation of the restaurant's owners and would never have aided her.

37. Can Samantha be convicted of solicitation?

(A) Yes, because the person approached need not accept the request for the crime of solicitation to be complete.

(B) Yes, because the person involved was a police officer.

(C) No, because the police officer would have never accepted her request for assistance.

(D) No, because Samantha did not manifest the state of mind of intent by simply asking a question.

Tony was in the hospital recovering from a recent fight with his neighbor, Pete. He and Pete have had many serious fights in the past, but this time, Tony sustained serious injuries because Pete hit him with a baseball bat. Tony wrote a letter to a friend, asking him to find Pete and inflict serious injuries upon him. Tony gave the letter to a nurse to be mailed, but the nurse left it lying on a table near the nurses' station. Later, Pete came over to visit Tony and to apologize about their previous altercation. Pete noticed the letter and grew suspicious that Tony was writing his friend following the fight. Pete opened the letter and discovered Tony's proposal to have him attacked.

38. Pete took the letter to the police. Can Tony be found guilty of solicitation?

(A) No, the letter never got to his friend, so he could not be guilty of soliciting a crime.

(B) No, Tony's letter only reflected a natural impulsive reaction to his situation and would not constitute a solicitation to commit a crime.

(C) Yes, the crime of solicitation was complete when Tony wrote the letter.

(D) Yes, as long as Tony intended the crime would take place and made some effort to effectuate that intent.

Two police officers, monitoring a street corner known for prostitution, observed a young, provocatively dressed woman waiving at passing cars, yelling "Hey baby, want some fun?" During the hour the officers observed her, she talked with several drivers in cars that pulled over, but the officers could not hear what was said. When the woman started to get into the vehicle of one of the men she had been speaking with, the officers arrested both of them. The woman blurted out, "I'm just trying to make some money."

39. Can the woman be found guilty of solicitation to prostitution?

(A) No, there is no direct evidence that a crime was being solicited.

(B) No, if the officers did not hear the conversation between the woman and the driver, the government will not be able to establish intent.

(C) Yes, the circumstantial evidence can establish that she was attempting to suggest a sexual encounter and the woman's comment establishes that it would be done in exchange for money.

(D) Yes, her behavior, dress, and suspicious location alone could establish that she was engaged in prostitution.

[B]   Attempt

After years of enduring abuse by his father, George began to consider killing him. He planned the murder for months, deciding to shoot him and dispose of the body in a remote lake near his family's mountain cabin. George wrote of all of this in his journal, including the dates and times he intended to carry out his plan. Two days before he and his father were to leave to go to the cabin, the father found the journal and read of his son's plans to murder him that very weekend. The father turned over the journal to the police who arrested George immediately.

40.   Can George be found guilty of attempted murder?

   (A)   No, because it is not clear that George really intended to murder his father.

   (B)   No, because George had not yet acted on his plan.

   (C)   Yes, because the plan to kill his father was now an imminent threat.

   (D)   Yes, because the plan constituted an action toward the murder.

A child was severely beaten by his father, resulting in severe brain trauma. The child only survived after prolonged medical treatment. His injuries were worsened by a significant delay in obtaining medical treatment.

41.   Regardless of the father's responsibility for the beating, can the mother, who behaved recklessly in failing to seek prompt medical treatment for the child's injuries, be convicted of attempted involuntary manslaughter?

   (A)   No, because the father's culpability in the child's injuries precludes prosecution of others.

   (B)   No, because the mother lacks the requisite mens rea for the charge.

   (C)   Yes, because her actions would have constituted involuntary manslaughter had the child died from his injuries.

   (D)   Yes, because the delay in treatment made the condition life threatening.

Ros was found parked in front of her boss's home early one evening. The next door neighbor testified that Ros had been waiting there for more than two hours. When arrested, Ros was searched. The police officers discovered a pistol in her purse.

42.   On these facts, can Ros be convicted of attempted murder?

ANSWER:

Doug decided to rob a bank. He planned the heist for several weeks and rented an apartment near the bank where he believed he could avoid detection for a few months before moving to a new city. He set a date for the robbery and found an accomplice who could break into the safe, but he had no clearly established plans yet for the details of the robbery. It turned out that this accomplice, the expert on safe cracking, was an undercover police officer, and Doug was immediately arrested for attempted armed robbery. Doug confessed to the plan.

43.   Can Doug be convicted of this crime without any other evidence?
ANSWER:

Julia broke into the home of her neighbor, an old enemy, and was going to shoot him while he was sleeping. Julia was unaware that her husband had earlier unloaded the gun, for fear that she would do something rash and kill someone. The neighbor awoke, saw Julia, and she ran out of his house.

44.   Can Julia be convicted of attempted murder even though the gun was unloaded?

    (A)   Yes, the fact that the gun was unloaded does not preclude a conviction of attempt.

    (B)   Yes, because Julia broke into the neighbor's house, she must have meant to kill him.

    (C)   No, because Julia may have only wanted to scare the neighbor.

    (D)   No, because there was no way under these circumstances that Julia could have killed the victim.

45.   Could Julia be convicted of attempted murder if the neighbor was not actually at home when Julia broke into the house?

    (A)   Yes, any action taken in furtherance of a planned crime constitutes an attempt.

    (B)   Yes, if Julia thought the neighbor was home when she broke in.

    (C)   No, it would have been impossible for Julia to shoot the neighbor that night.

    (D)   No, Julia's crime here was burglary, not attempted murder.

Rebecca had been caring for her elderly aunt for some months now, hoping to eventually recover a large portion of her aunt's considerable estate. Growing impatient with her situation, and eager to collect on her aunt's will as soon as possible, Rebecca replaced her aunt's vitamins with lethal poison. When her aunt remained unaffected by the new pills, Rebecca learned that she had given the aunt a harmless herbal supplement rather than the lethal drug. Feeling remorseful about her evil motives, Rebecca then decided to just wait for her aunt's natural end.

46.   Has she committed attempted murder?

    (A)   Yes, because society has an interest in punishing people's bad thoughts.

    (B)   Yes, because Rebecca had the intent to kill her aunt and took a substantial act toward the commission of the crime.

    (C)   No, because Rebecca's decision not to go through with her plan precludes prosecution for attempted murder.

    (D)   No, because there is no way the herbal supplement could have been lethal.

[C] Conspiracy

Sybil and John agreed to kidnap the daughter of a local politician and hold her for ransom. Their plan succeeded, and they released the child after receiving the money. They were apprehended several days later.

47.   Under the majority rule, can each of them be convicted of—and sentenced for—both kidnapping and conspiracy to commit the kidnapping?

    (A)   Yes, because conspiracy does not merge with the completed offense, so convictions for both the completed offense and conspiracy to commit that offense would be allowed.

    (B)   No, because the conspiracy and the crime share the same objectives, merger of the two offenses is required.

    (C)   No, because like the other inchoate offenses of solicitation and attempt, conspiracy merges with the completed offense if the completed offense is a felony.

    (D)   No, because punishing Sybil and John for both crimes would violate the constitutional ban against double jeopardy.

Erika and Lauren went into a convenience store to buy some sodas and snacks. When they entered the store, they browsed the aisles a bit and noticed that no one was attending the cash register. Erika went behind the counter and started trying to open the cash register. Erika exchanged brief eye contact with her friend. Lauren said nothing, but she giggled a bit and looked around nervously. Erika managed to get the cash register open, filled her pockets with the cash, and started running out of the store with Lauren. The two young women were in the parking lot when the owner of the shop came from the back room, realized what had occurred, and telephoned the police. Erika and Lauren were caught several minutes later.

48.   Can they be convicted of conspiracy to commit theft?

    (A)   Yes, because there was an explicit agreement to commit the crime.

    (B)   Yes, because there was an implied understanding and no explicit agreement is required for a conspiracy.

    (C)   No, because there was no explicit agreement to commit the crime.

    (D)   No, because Lauren did not do anything to suggest she was in agreement.

Kate and her sister Emily were not on the best of terms. At their cousin's wedding, Kate's sister humiliated her in front of their entire family. Kate sat outside the party thinking of how to get back at her sister, when Emily's husband Thomas approached her. Kate and Thomas talked for hours, discussing Emily's malevolent nature. Finally, Thomas suggested that Kate should hire someone to really hurt and scare Emily. He said it would teach Emily a lesson, Kate would feel vindicated, and the sisters would finally be able to put the past behind them. Kate would have to take the lead role, Thomas explained, as he and Emily had been having so many marital problems, he would be immediately under suspicion. He said he would, however, be happy to do much of the planning. Kate was shocked to hear her brother-in-law suggest such a thing and she said nothing. Thomas continued to elaborate on his proposal, and Kate said she agreed to the plan, although she never would really consider harming Emily in such a way. Over the next few days, Thomas discussed with Kate having Emily "roughed up" by someone because she had made everybody's life so miserable. Uncertain of how to proceed, Kate called the police to tell them of Thomas' plans. The police instructed Kate to act as if she planned to carry out the crime. Thomas made further arrangements for Emily's beating. When he met with Kate to instruct her how to contact "the thug" he had located, their conversation was covertly recorded and Thomas was soon arrested.

49. According to the modern trend, can Thomas be convicted of a conspiracy offense?

(A) Yes, because Thomas believed himself to be acting pursuant to an agreement with Kate.

(B) Yes, because there was an agreement by Thomas and Kate to have Emily beaten.

(C) No, because Kate never intended to carry out the agreement, there was no true agreement.

(D) No, because Thomas could not carry out his plan without Kate's agreement and subsequent actions.

Joel, an undercover drug agent, visited the apartment of Betty, a reputed dealer in marijuana. Betty agreed to sell Joel a quantity of drugs; she divided his portion from a large amount she had on hand. Unable to find a container for it, she called to her boyfriend, Zeb, and asked if he had any plastic bags. From the bedroom, Zeb responded that she could find some bags in the kitchen pantry. Betty located the bags and completed the sale of marijuana to Joel. Betty was convicted of distribution of an illegal substance.

50. Under the majority rule, could her deal with Joel give rise to a conspiracy conviction for Betty?

(A) Yes, because the requirements of intent, agreement, and action in furtherance of that agreement are satisfied.

(B) No, because Joel was an undercover officer and therefore was not really intending to buy the drugs.

(C) No, because Betty has already been convicted of the substantive offense of distribution.

(D) No, because Joel's actions constitute entrapment, providing Betty a complete defense.

51. Under the facts above, could Zeb be convicted of conspiracy?

ANSWER:

Reggie often hung out on the street in front of Karry's convenience store. Reggie occasionally came in for purchases when he had some money. One night, he came in with a group of teenagers and bought a large quantity of beer. He began to come in with the kids every week or so. Karry received a notice from the alcohol regulatory board that underage purchasers might be buying alcohol through other purchasers, pointing out that kids had been approaching people with little money to entice them into purchasing alcohol on their behalf. For the next few weeks, Reggie came in every few days and bought a large quantity of beer, each time with the teenagers next to him. One day, an undercover police officer was in the store, and after questioning the group, he determined that Reggie was purchasing alcohol for the teenagers.

52. While Karry's license to sell alcoholic beverages will certainly be reviewed, could she also face criminal liability for conspiracy?

    (A) No, because there is no evidence that Karry had an agreement with Reggie.

    (B) No, because Karry committed no crime in selling the alcohol to Reggie, as he is of legal age.

    (C) No, because the crime of conspiracy requires a criminal intent.

    (D) Yes, because an agreement to commit a crime could be inferred from her relationship with Reggie.

Eddie was leaving a concert one night when he saw Marco, a guy who owed him money. Eddie said to his friends, "Hey, we gotta get that guy," and he and his friends chased Marco down and attacked him. The group forced Marco to the ground, punching and kicking him and yelling that he had better pay Eddie. Marco tried to run away from his attackers. Confused and disoriented, he ran into the street without looking. Marco was hit by a car and died several hours later at the hospital.

53. Can Eddie and his friends be convicted of conspiracy to commit murder?

    (A) Yes, because their intent and agreement to attack Marco is clear from their actions.

    (B) Yes, because their behavior demonstrates their actions as reckless, allowing a conviction of murder as well as a conviction of conspiracy to commit murder.

    (C) No, it is not clear that Eddie's group agreed to any plan, so they cannot be held responsible for conspiracy.

    (D) No, because they did not demonstrate the necessary intent to carry out the crime of conspiracy to commit murder.

Catherine and Steve supplemented their income while in college by distributing methamphet-amine. Their operation was fairly small-scale. Steve usually purchased a quantity from a dealer in a nearby town, although Catherine provided the original contact, and the couple sold mostly to students they knew. When Steve began using drugs heavily, their relationship went sour, and they split apart. Catherine graduated from college and was working for three years at a consulting firm. Never telling Steve her plans, she had no significant contact with Steve during the three-year period. Catherine was eager to put that earlier period of her life behind her and stayed clear of the drug scene entirely. Steve's path was much different. He found himself deeply in debt shortly after Catherine left, and he began increasing his operations in order to pay back his creditors and supplement his own drug habit. After Catherine left, Steve found a few other individuals to work with in the operation. Unfortunately for Steve, one of those people was an undercover police officer.

54. If Steve and his circle of contacts in the drug world are convicted of conspiracy to distribute illegal substances, could Catherine also be convicted?

    (A) Yes, because Catherine took part in the criminal enterprise from the beginning and would be responsible for all later actions.

    (B) Yes, because the foreseeable actions of one conspirator can be attributed to another.

    (C) No, because Steve's actions were unforeseeable.

    (D) No, because Catherine had distanced herself from the operation for some time.

Assume that, before she left, Catherine tried to help Steve get out of the drug business and go to a rehabilitation center. She even told him of her plans. She also contacted the school and the police officials anonymously to inform them of Steve's conduct.

55. In most jurisdictions, would this absolve her of liability for the later criminal acts?

    (A) Yes, because Catherine withdrew from the criminal enterprise.

    (B) Yes, because she made it clear that her role in the scheme was over.

    (C) No, because the crime of conspiracy was already complete.

    (D) No, because she was an essential part of the conspiracy at its inception.

56. What if, at the time of Steve's prosecution, Catherine had been uninvolved for three and a half years. The statute of limitations on the conspiracy charge is three years. Can Catherine still be prosecuted?

    (A) Yes, because the crime had not been discovered until after the statute of limitations had tolled.

    (B) Yes, because the conspiracy continued to operate, so the statue of limitations had not begun to toll.

    (C) No, because one cannot be charged with a crime for actions taken after the statute of limitations has run.

(D) No, because she had not been involved and therefore cannot be charged for the crimes of others.

Cooper and Jackson were two prisoners who shared a common dislike for their fellow prisoner, Sheldon. One day, in the cafeteria, Jackson noticed Cooper backing Sheldon in the corner and threatening him. Cooper and Sheldon began to argue, and Sheldon punched Cooper in the stomach. Jackson ran over to the fight. Jackson and Cooper both started punching and kicking Sheldon. Suddenly, Cooper pulled out a rudimentary knife he had made and stabbed Sheldon twice. Jackson merely stood there as the stabbing occurred.

57. Can Jackson be charged with the crime of conspiracy to commit murder if Sheldon dies? The crime of murder?

ANSWER:

Gabe and Jessie agreed that they would form a group to import, keep, and sell illegal drugs. After renting a truck to use when picking up the drugs from the dock, the two were arrested. They have been charged, under a general conspiracy statute, with three federal offenses: Conspiracy to import, conspiracy to possess, and conspiracy to distribute.

58. Can they be convicted of the three conspiracy offenses?

(A) Yes, Gabe and Jessie agreed to acts that would have violated three different criminal statutes.

(B) Yes, a conspiracy may be broken into distinct crimes when linked with distinct statutes had their actions been successful.

(C) No, renting a truck was too insubstantial an act in furtherance of the plot.

(D) No, a single agreement cannot be broken into separate conspiracy charges under one general conspiracy statute.

59. Would the answer change if Gabe and Jessie were prosecuted under three separate and distinct conspiracy statutes?

(A) Yes, for it would prove three separate and distinct agreements.

(B) Yes, for it would demonstrate the legislature's intent that one agreement could be broken into separate conspiracy prosecutions.

(C) No, for one agreement can only be the basis for one conspiracy prosecution.

(D) No, for such a prosecution would violate Double Jeopardy principles.

[A]   The Property Offenses: Larceny, Embezzlement, False Pretenses

While shopping in an upscale boutique, John came across a cashmere coat that he had to have. It was impeccably tailored and the perfect color. Of course, it was priced accordingly. John slipped off his own inexpensive jacket and put on the coat. He went into the dressing room to try it on, where he also stopped to rip off the security sensor and price tag. He continued to browse through the shop a bit and made his way toward the exit, looking around him to be sure no one was taking notice. A few steps out on the street, John was stopped by a security guard. He was subsequently arrested for larceny.

60.   Has John committed larceny?

(A)   Yes, because he intended to steal the coat and left the premises.

(B)   No, because he intended to steal, but was unsuccessful.

(C)   No, because he was not trespassing.

(D)   No, because while he left the store, he was still in the vicinity of it.

Juanita was the manager of the flower store. As such, she had full responsibility for ordering and pricing goods, hiring and firing employees, and promoting the store generally. One day she took home a fancy plant, sold it to her friend, and kept the money.

61.   What crime has she committed?

(A)   Embezzlement.

(B)   Larceny.

(C)   False pretenses.

(D)   Robbery.

Amy was visiting one of her favorite cities. She went to dinner at a famed restaurant and enjoyed an extravagant, four-course meal, complete with a bottle of very expensive wine. When the check came, she reached into her purse and realized she had forgotten her wallet back in her hotel room. She panicked, and decided that the meal would have been more than she could afford anyway. She gathered her things, headed for the restroom, and exited out a service entrance, never paying her bill.

62.   Has Amy committed larceny?

ANSWER:

27

Thomas worked for a large bank managing trusts for wealthy clients. He personally invested his money conservatively and did not often buy large quantities of stock. Marta, a friend from college, called him one afternoon and talked with him at length about a young biotech company for which Marta worked. She mentioned some things about this company that convinced Thomas that it would be incredibly profitable within five years. Thomas also learned from another source that this company was about to have a public offering. Unfortunately, Thomas' assets were not "liquid," and by the time he would be able to raise enough capital, the opportunity to invest would be lost. Thomas decided to skew the numbers at work a bit and borrow some cash from the bank in order to purchase shares in this company. He knew he could return the money within a short time if all went well.

63. If Thomas' dealings came to light some time later, could he be found guilty of embezzlement?

   (A) Yes, even if Thomas was able to return the money, he still embezzled from the company.

   (B) Yes, but if Thomas actually returned the money before he was caught, he will not be convicted.

   (C) No, because Thomas was not acting as an employee at the time.

   (D) No, if he returned the funds, subsequently, he would not be found guilty because he was only temporarily borrowing the money.

Daniel's job involved marketing corporate contracts for a national cellular communications company. In the course of his job, he often provided free phones and discounted service, on a discretionary basis, to important people working for his corporate clients. As such, he usually had many expensive, advanced mobile phones in his possession and the ability to vouch for discounts on service, with very little oversight from his telecom company. As a favor to a friend, Daniel gave her a new, free phone and provided her with discounted service, although this was merely a personal friend who did not have any connections with his corporate clients. When his supervisor discovered this favor, Daniel was fired.

64. Can Daniel be found guilty of embezzlement?

   (A) No, because he did not intend to embezzle from the company.

   (B) No, because he was merely providing equipment to people, not taking money.

   (C) Yes, because the statute likely encompasses the taking or conversion of property as well as money.

   (D) Yes, because the company for which he worked had fired him for abuse of his discretion.

After being unemployed for a couple of months, Stephanie was ready to take almost any employment she could find. Sitting at a neighborhood bar one evening, another patron named Gary told her about a great money making opportunity if Stephanie would help him set up a new business. All that was required was that Stephanie call potential investors to see if they would be interested in establishing a new retirement community on the edge of town.

As Gary explained it to Stephanie, the development would be run like a condominium, with all of the residents being involved from the earliest stages of the project, in order to maximize each person's retirement dreams. Once a threshold of investors was brought in, the investors themselves could decide decisions on planning and amenities, so they could actually shape their future community themselves. Stephanie thought this sounded like a great idea, and she wanted a job. She called area seniors with this exact information given to her by Gary, indicating that the property had been purchased and preliminary roads put in, but the remainder of the project depended on individual contributions. Stephanie raised thousands of dollars within a couple of weeks and was paid handsomely for her success. An investigation by area law enforcement revealed that Gary had purchased no land in the area and was merely taking the money from the project's investors.

65. Can Stephanie now be found guilty of false presences?

    (A) Yes, because Stephanie misrepresented to her clients a material fact.

    (B) Yes, because Stephanie was involved in a criminal operation to defraud area seniors.

    (C) No, because Stephanie did not have knowledge that the misrepresentations were false.

    (D) No, because if there was a misrepresentation, it was of a future fact (i.e., that the community would be built), not of a past or present fact.

[B] Offenses Against the Habitation: Burglary, Arson

Amanda was at home and turned on the TV to watch the seven o'clock news. She heard someone on her porch. Thinking it was her fiancé, she opened the front door. On her porch was a strange man who demanded she let him in the house. When she refused, he pulled out a gun. Amanda, fearful for her life, let him in. Once inside, he searched the house for valuables, took her engagement ring and cash from a drawer. He then left the house.

66. Has this man committed burglary?

    (A) Yes, because he constructively met all of the requirements for burglary.

    (B) Yes, because he robbed her in her home.

    (C) No, because he did not commit a breaking to gain entry.

    (D) No, because the crime occurred early in the evening.

67. What result if the incident took place at 3 p.m. not 7 p.m.?

    (A) Same result at common law.

    (B) Different result at common law.

    (C) Same result under most modern statutes.

    (D) Different result under most modern statutes.

Curtis was drunk when he decided to drive outside of town. On his way out of town, Curtis flung his lit cigarette butt out the window of his vehicle. The cigarette caused a huge forest fire that destroyed many homes. The fire was finally put out by a heavy storm three days later.

    68.   Can Curtis be convicted of arson?

ANSWER:

Nicolena hated her next-door neighbor. Plotting to burn down the neighbor's house (so that he would move away), Nicolena planted an explosive device on the wall of the neighbor's home. The plan was that device would explode, and the house would then catch fire and burn down. The device was set off and it did explode. It caused extensive damage, but it did not actually cause anything to catch fire.

    69.   Can Nicolena be found guilty of arson?

       (A)   Yes, Nicolena intentionally damaged the house.

       (B)   No, Nicolena never entered the neighbor's house.

       (C)   No, arson can be found only if the residence is entirely destroyed.

       (D)   No, arson can be found only if some part of the residence catches fire.

[C] Homicide

[1] Killing

Sam hated Keesha because she was more popular than he. One evening, he grabbed Keesha and threw her into a car. Sam drove to a remote location and shot Keesha. Amazingly, Keesha was found alive and taken to a hospital. Keesha lay in a coma as a result of the gunshot and died 395 days later.

    70.   Under the common law, is Sam guilty of murder?

       (A)   Yes, because Sam had the intent to kill Keesha and she died as a result of his actions.

       (B)   No, because Keesha died too long after she was shot.

       (C)   No, because Sam only wanted to hurt Keesha, not kill her; he hoped that someone would find her.

       (D)   No, because Sam was clearly crazy; a sane person would not shoot another person in this situation.

Jane snuck into John's house in the middle of the night and shot him twice while he appeared to be sleeping. Unbeknownst to Jane, John was already dead because Fritz put poison in John's wine at dinner earlier that night.

71. Is Jane guilty of murder since she had the intent to kill John and actually shot him?

    (A) No, because Jane did not cause John's death.

    (B) No, because Jane's actions might not have killed John if he had been alive.

    (C) Yes, because Jane had the intent to kill John and committed the act.

    (D) Yes, because Jane should be punished for her actions just the same as if John had been alive.

Jill told Jack that they were going to have a baby. Jack was not pleased to learn that he was going to be a father. Five months later, Jack punched Jill in the abdomen several times, saying that he hoped the baby would die. Jill immediately went into labor and gave birth to a girl.

72. In order to convict Jack of murder under the common law, does it matter if the baby was born alive and died minutes later, or if she was stillborn?

    (A) No, because in both cases Jack had the intent to kill and committed the act resulting in the baby's death.

    (B) No. Jack cannot be found guilty of murder in either case because the act in both cases was committed before the baby's birth.

    (C) No. In both cases there may have been other reasons why the baby died.

    (D) Yes. A baby must be born alive for a person to be found guilty of murder, which involves the killing of a person.

73. Would your previous answer be different in states that have introduced feticide statutes?

ANSWER:

James was seriously injured in a car accident when the driver of another car swerved into his lane. After being transported to the hospital, James's heart was still beating. Nonetheless, he was connected to a respirator, was being tube-fed, but exhibited no reflexes or brain stem activity.

74. If the doctors disconnect him from life-support, is the driver of the car that hit James guilty of a homicide offense under modern statutes?

    (A) No, because James's heart was beating at the time of the doctors' actions.

    (B) No, because the doctors killed James when they turned off the life-support.

    (C) Yes, because James was brain dead.

    (D) No, because a homicide offense cannot be based on a car accident.

[2] Murder

Amy and Bess were good friends until Bess "stole" Amy's boyfriend Bernardo a month ago. Amy wanted to "remove Bess from the picture." Amy saw Bess at the mall and talked things over. Amy said she forgave Bess for going out with Bernardo. Friends once again, they went out driving together. Amy began speeding down the road, shouting into the wind with exhilaration. Amy wrapped her car around a telephone pole while driving at speeds in excess of 130 m.p.h. Bess was killed in the crash.

75. Is Amy guilty of murder?

   (A) Yes, because driving at such high speeds shows a complete disregard for the safety of others.

   (B) Yes, because Amy previously had the intent to kill Bess.

   (C) No, because Bess voluntarily got in the car with Amy.

   (D) No, because Amy was having fun and did not stop to think that they might be in an accident.

Jolinda had severe muscular dystrophy. Michael was a nurse paid through a trust fund to take care of Jolinda. Authorities recently found Jolinda in an appalling condition. She appeared emaciated, with sores from lying in bed for several weeks straight. Although the police took Jolinda straight to the hospital, she could not be saved and died a few days later from malnutrition.

76. Under the common law, would Michael be guilty of murder?

   (A) No, because he had no duty to act.

   (B) No, because he did not commit any act that resulted in Jolinda's death.

   (C) Yes, because he was obligated to take care of Jolinda and failed to do so.

   (D) Yes, because it is inhumane to leave someone in such a condition.

Leonard's upstairs neighbor was a grumpy woman with a serious heart condition. She called the police whenever Leonard had a party and yelled that his television was too loud. She also reported him to the landlord for propping open the outer door to the apartment building. Leonard could not stand his neighbor and devised a plan to get rid of her permanently. First, Leonard appeared to befriend his elderly neighbor. He began offering to carry her groceries up the stairs and he spoke to her politely. He even kept his television volume turned down. He knew that the woman's daughter came by every Sunday promptly at 2:00 p.m. One Sunday, he caught the woman's daughter entering the building and told her that her mother wanted her to pick up a few items at the store. When he handed her a list, the daughter left the building. After waiting a short time, Leonard went to the woman's apartment. She told him that she was worried because her daughter is never late. He responded that "the police just came 'round. Your daughter was in a car accident on the way here; she's dead. I told them you should hear this from a friend." The old woman sunk to the floor, crying. Then she clutched her chest and gasped for breath. Pleased that his plan worked so well, Leonard stood and watched as she died.

77.   Is Leonard guilty of murder?

ANSWER:

Abdul and Eric had never met before, but they were in the same café when a brawl started. Caught up in the mayhem, Abdul swung wildly and punched Eric in the face. Eric died from the injuries.

78.   Is Abdul guilty of murder?

(A)   No, because Abdul did not intend to kill Eric.

(B)   No, because Abdul did not have the necessary state of mind for murder.

(C)   Yes, because Abdul intended to commit serious bodily injury to Eric.

(D)   Yes, because Abdul acted recklessly.

79.   Suppose Abdul was a giant of a man, 6'5" tall, weighing about 300 pounds and was a former professional boxer. Would the result be different?

ANSWER:

A man went into a public library and stole an unattended book bag. As he was slowly driving his car out of the library parking lot, he accidentally hit a pedestrian and killed her.

80.   Is the man guilty of murder?

(A)   No, because the man did not intend to hit the pedestrian.

(B)   No, because larceny of a book bag is not an inherently dangerous felony.

(C)   Yes, because the man killed the pedestrian while leaving a crime scene.

(D)   Yes, because the man could not have hit a pedestrian without being grossly reckless.

81.   Would the man be guilty of murder if, instead of stealing an unattended book bag, he took the book bag from its owner at gunpoint before accidentally hitting the pedestrian?

(A)   No, because it was an accident.

(B)   No, because the robbery was completed prior to killing the pedestrian.

(C)   Yes, because the pedestrian was killed during the commission of a violent felony.

(D) Yes, because the pedestrian died as a result of being hit by the thief's car.

Sylvia ran after committing an armed robbery. As she went down the street, a policeman aimed his gun at her and fired. The policeman's bullet accidentally killed an innocent bystander.

82. Is Sylvia liable for the homicide?
ANSWER:

83. Suppose Sylvia, while trying to escape, took a hostage and used him as a shield. Officers then fired at Sylvia and they killed the hostage. Is Sylvia guilty of felony murder?
ANSWER:

In anger, Justin assaulted Patrice. Patrice died from the injuries sustained during the attack.

84. In most jurisdictions, could Justin be convicted of murder using the felony murder rule?

(A) No, because the assault would merge with the homicide.

(B) No, because Justin could be convicted of murder on other grounds.

(C) Yes, because assault is a dangerous felony.

(D) Yes, because the felony murder rule eliminates the need to demonstrate malice.

One night after everyone else had gone home for the night, Ronald and Janie started a fire in order to burn down their office building to collect insurance proceeds. As they walked down the alley back to Ronald's car, a policeman on patrol stepped out of the shadows and asked them for identification. Ronald and Janie pulled out guns and ran down the alley into the street. Janie wildly fired a shot back toward the alley, thinking that she would stop the policeman. Instead, Janie's bullet killed a pedestrian who was watching the burning building. The police officer ran after Janie and shot her, killing her.

85. Is Ronald guilty of murdering the bystander? Of murdering Janie?
ANSWER:

The defendant in a felony murder prosecution offered testimony indicating that the prosecution evidence as to the necessary state of mind for the underlying dangerous felony—armed robbery—might be lacking. As a consequence, the judge gave the following instruction to the jury:

In order to convict for the crime of felony murder in our jurisdiction, you must find that the government has proven, beyond a reasonable doubt, that the death of the victim here occurred during the commission of the armed robbery of him by the defendant. In addition, you must find that the elements of the crime of armed robbery have been shown by the government beyond a reasonable doubt.

86.   On appeal, should the court find error?

(A)   No, the instruction correctly states the jury's obligation in a felony murder prosecution.

(B)   No, while it did not correctly state the law, any resulting harm was not prejudicial.

(C)   Yes, the jury is not required to make any finding as to the armed robbery.

(D)   Yes, the jury is not required to find, beyond a reasonable doubt, the elements of the crime of armed robbery.

Hannibal carefully selected his victims. He singled out people whom he felt treated him unfairly or rudely in the past. He claimed to have eaten his victims after slowly killing them.

87.   If he is telling the truth, of which crime is Hannibal guilty?

(A)   First degree murder because the killings were premeditated.

(B)   First degree murder because the killings were done with malice.

(C)   Second degree murder because the killings were done with malice.

(D)   Voluntary manslaughter because his victims provoked Hannibal.

For over a year, Mary had been planning to kill Vince. One night, she at last carried out her plan with a single gunshot to the head.

88.   Of what homicide crime is Mary guilty?

(A)   First degree murder because the killing was done with premeditation.

(B)   First degree murder because Mary intended to kill Vince.

(C)   Second degree murder because the crime was not gruesome or heinous.

(D)   Second degree murder because Mary intended to kill Vince.

The government in a gruesome killing case sought a conviction for first degree murder. It requested that the trial judge give this instruction to the jury as to the necessary state of mind:

An intent to kill, plus premeditation and deliberation, may be formed only moments before the fatal act is committed provided the accused had time to think and did intend to kill.

89.   Should the judge instruct the jury in this way?

ANSWER:

Spouses Bill and Juanita took a trip to Colorado. Several weeks later, Juanita came back into town without Bill and told her friends that Bill left her on the trip. Juanita was seen around town with several young men after she returned. Neighbors say that Bill and Juanita argued often before the trip. His friends say that he had never suggested that he wanted to leave Juanita. Authorities find that Juanita took out an extremely large life insurance policy on Bill just before leaving for Colorado. Bill has not used his credit cards or accessed his bank accounts since the Colorado trip. Although Bill normally called his son (who lives with his ex-wife) every night and kept in very regular contact with a circle of buddies, neither his friends nor his family have heard from him. Authorities suspect that Juanita killed Bill to collect the insurance money.

90. Can Juanita be convicted of murder even if Bill's body is never found?

   (A) Yes, because Juanita had a motive to kill Bill.

   (B) Yes, because there is evidence to prove Juanita killed Bill.

   (C) No, because there must be a body to prove that a homicide occurred.

   (D) No, because there is only circumstantial evidence linking Juanita to the crime.

[3] Manslaughter

Joe and his fiancé Sarah got into a huge fight in the grocery store parking lot. Sarah slapped him and called him nasty names. Joe then seemed to go berserk. He screamed at her, took out a knife he always carried and stabbed her in the chest. She died a few days later from the stabbing.

91. Of what type of homicide is Joe guilty?

ANSWER:

92. Would your previous answer change if Joe did not immediately stab Sarah? Instead, Joe went home, "stewed" about his anger for a few days, then charged to Sarah's house and stabbed her to death.

ANSWER:

Tim's 6-year-old daughter Anna had a fever for several days. Although he had been giving her aspirin, her fever continued to rise. Anna's fever got to 105 and she began to shake visibly. Tim did not have much money and did not have medical insurance, so he continued to put off taking his daughter to the doctor, out of embarrassment.

93. If Anna died the next day, is Tim guilty of manslaughter?

   (A) No, because he had no duty to act.

(B) No, because he was treating her as well as he knew how.

(C) Yes, because he was obligated to get medical attention for Anna and did not.

(D) Yes, because his inability to pay for treatment provoked him to act irrationally.

94. Suppose Tim disregarded advice from his friend, a pediatrician, that he was putting his daughter in serious danger by not bringing her immediately to a doctor. Could he then be convicted of murder instead of involuntary manslaughter?

(A) No, the risk is still not great enough.

(B) No, a defendant cannot be found guilty of murder unless he intended to kill or cause great bodily harm.

(C) Yes, even without the advice Tim would be guilty of murder.

(D) Yes, the risk in such a situation is so great and obvious as to allow the charge to be murder.

Jerome and Francine had been married three years. One day at the grocery store, Jerome was picking up some food. A man whom he had never met came up to him and said, "Francine and I have been having an affair. She is going to leave you and come live with me." For a few moments, Jerome stood in disbelief. Suddenly Jerome grabbed a frozen turkey from a nearby bin and swung it at the man while screaming, "I'm going to kill you both!" Jerome hit the man on the head several times before running out of the store. The man died soon after from the injuries.

95. Is Jerome guilty of manslaughter?

ANSWER:

Patrick started taking a new medication on Friday. The doctor and the pharmacist each warned him not to drive while taking the medicine. The medicine bottle had a prominent label warning against operating machinery, including motor vehicles. Patrick noticed that he had been dropping off to sleep all weekend. Nevertheless, he got into his car Monday morning to go to work. There was a construction zone on the highway, so the heavy traffic was moving rather slowly. Patrick fell asleep and veered into a car in the next lane. That car swerved and screeched to a stop as it slammed into the concrete construction barricade. Despite the slow speeds, the driver of the other car was killed.

96. Of what crime is Patrick guilty?

(A) Murder; driving in that condition was gross recklessness.

(B) Involuntary manslaughter; he was criminally reckless.

(C) No crime; he was negligent, but not reckless.

(D) No crime; the danger was not foreseeable.

[D] Kidnapping

Felicia decided to kidnap her boss Pablo in order to hold him for a ransom. While Pablo was supervising the clothing section of the large department store where they both worked, Felicia put a knife to his back and demanded that he walk slowly out to the public parking lot across the street from the store. As soon as they got to the parking lot, a police officer observed what was going on, became suspicious, and arrested Felicia.

97. Can Felicia be convicted of the crime of kidnapping?

   (A) Yes, once she put the knife to Pablo's back and demanded that he move, the crime was complete.

   (B) Yes, the crime was complete as soon as Pablo left the place where he wished to remain.

   (C) No, Felicia was never able to get Pablo away from the area by the store.

   (D) No, without the use of actual force against the victim, the kidnapping was not complete.

98. What would the result be if Felicia did not use force against Pablo but told him that if he did not go with her, her associate would beat his elderly mother right then?

   (A) Same result; force directed against any person is sufficient for the crime.

   (B) Same result; no force need be shown for the crime.

   (C) Different result; it is only a crime if the force is directed against the person moved.

   (D) Different result; mere threat of force is insufficient for the crime.

99. Suppose that Felicia only kept Pablo in the parking lot for a minute, then had a change of heart and released him. Would she be guilty of a kidnapping?

   (A) No, that would be too short a time for the victim's confinement.

   (B) No, it is only a kidnapping based on a limited confinement if the victim suffers some physical injury.

   (C) Yes, any appreciable period of time for the confinement satisfies the element of the crime.

   (D) Yes, the crime was complete when Felicia threatened Pablo.

Taylor came up to Professor Hortense after class and demanded that she remain in the classroom after all the students left. She resisted doing so, at which point Taylor told her, "Look, I have a loaded pistol in my back pack. If you don't stay here for another 10 minutes or so, I will shoot you." The professor remained for 10 minutes while Taylor yelled at her about her poor teaching. After 10 minutes, Taylor allowed her to leave.

100. Did Taylor kidnap the professor?

ANSWER:

[E] Robbery

Jennie approached a man on a city sidewalk. Showing him a toy gun she had concealed beneath her coat, she demanded that he give her his travel bag and money. The man, fearful, quickly complied.

101. Has Jennie committed robbery?

(A) Yes, because she stole his bag and money.

(B) Yes, because the fact that the gun was fake is no defense to the charge of robbery.

(C) No, because the defendant was unable to harm him with a gun.

(D) No, because the defendant committed no violence against the victim.

Pickpocket Paul smoothly took the victim's wallet from her back pocket.

102. Has Paul committed the crime of robbery?

ANSWER:

[F] Sex Offenses

Lance and Sheena were at a party. Sheena was a petite woman, weighing just 105 pounds. Body builder Lance weighed well over 200 pounds. Sheena drank more than she could handle and went to an upstairs bedroom for a nap. Lance saw Sheena go upstairs. Twenty minutes later, he went up and saw that she was asleep in the bed. He took off his clothes, and without saying anything, began to fondle Sheena's body. Sheena awoke, and "froze," saying and doing nothing. She later testified that she did nothing because she was terrified that Lance would harm her if she did. Lance then inserted his penis inside Sheena and ejaculated.

103. Is Lance guilty of the crime of rape?

(A) No, Lance did not realize that Sheena did not wish to have intercourse with him.

(B) No, Sheena's silence could be taken as consent to the act.

(C) Yes, Sheena did not consent to the act.

(D) Yes, Sheena did not expressly consent to the act.

104. Did Lance's action constitute intercourse by force or threat of force?

ANSWER:

Graduate student Alice was studying late in a remote part of the library one night. Professor Bob saw her and sat down next to her. He put his hand on her knee and she pushed it away. Bob told her that she had to have intercourse with him, for if she did not he would have her student scholarship revoked. Bob then had sexual intercourse with Alice without any voiced objection by Alice.

105.   In most jurisdictions, can Bob be convicted of the crime of rape?

(A)   No, because Bob did not use physical force.

(B)   No, because Alice did not expressly object to the sexual act.

(C)   Yes, because rape is now understood to include coercive acts.

(D)   Yes, because Alice demonstrated a clear lack of consent.

Brandon is 23 years old. Cate is 17 years old. Brandon and Cate met at a college party. Cate's friends are all in college, and Cate routinely used a fake ID to buy alcohol. Given the circumstances, Brandon believed that Cate is 21 years old. Brandon asked Cate out on a few dates. On one of these dates, when Cate's parents were out of town, Cate invited Brandon over and they had sex. The age of consent in this jurisdiction is 18.

106.   Is Brandon guilty of rape under the modern approach to rape law?

(A)   No, because Cate consented.

(B)   No, because Brandon has a defense of reasonable mistake.

(C)   Yes, because Cate is under the age of consent.

(D)   Yes, because Brandon had the necessary state of mind for the crime.

Husband Hall, over the express objection of wife Wanda, threw Wanda on their bed and had sexual intercourse with her.

107.   Is Hall guilty of the crime of rape?

(A)   No, husbands cannot, as a matter of law, be convicted of raping their wives.

(B)   No, throwing Wanda on the bed is not sufficient to constitute force or threat of force.

(C)   Yes, if all the elements of the crime are otherwise shown.

(D)   Yes, the marital status of Hall and Wanda is utterly irrelevant to the prosecution.

108.   Can a man be found guilty of raping another man?
ANSWER:

Jerald and Gina moved in together about a year after they had started dating. They regularly engaged in sexual intercourse. The police had a valid search warrant and entered Jerald and

Gina's home. During the course of the search of the home, the police saw Gina and Jerald having sex in the bedroom. Jerald and Gina are afraid they will be charged with the crime of fornication.

109. Should they be concerned?

    (A) No, because fornication laws have been ruled unconstitutional.

    (B) No, because fornication laws have been repealed or abandoned in most states.

    (C) Yes, because the elements of the crime of fornication were met.

    (D) Yes, because the search violated constitutional rights.

Peter and James went fishing in Peter's boat. Peter said that there was better fishing over by the dam. James, concerned, pointed out the signs saying, "DANGER—Do not fish near dam." Peter insisted and stopped the boat near the dam. They spent the rest of the afternoon fishing there. After several packs of beer, James became drunk, fell overboard and drowned.

110. By fishing near the danger signs, is Peter guilty of involuntary manslaughter?

(A) Yes, because Peter insisted on illegally fishing in an unsafe location.

(B) Yes, because Peter is responsible for all results of his illegal act.

(C) No, because the cause of James' drowning was his being drunk.

(D) No, because James assumed the risk.

Anne lured Steve to a vacant office building in the upper midwest. When Steve arrived, Anne surprised him and tied him up. Anne told Steve that she wanted him to suffer and left Steve tied up. Anne only intended to leave Steve there for a few hours to scare him. While Anne was gone, a rattlesnake bit Steve. Steve died as a result.

111. Is Anne guilty of involuntary manslaughter?

(A) Yes, because Anne's behavior was negligent.

(B) Yes, because Anne's behavior was grossly reckless.

(C) No, because Steve dying from a rattlesnake bite was not foreseeable.

(D) No, because Anne did not intend to kill Steve.

112. Would the result change if—while tied up—Steve became terrified he would be left there forever, and began breathing heavily, ultimately dying from a heart attack?

ANSWER:

Jessie brutally beat up her enemy Flo. The beating was so bad that Flo was hospitalized and was advised by her doctor that even with surgery, her face would remain horribly disfigured. One hour later, Flo pulled out the feeding tubes that had previously been inserted in her body. The nurses did not discover this until later in the day when Flo was already dead.

113.   Is Jessie guilty of a homicide offense?

   (A)   Yes, her action foreseeably resulted in Flo's death.

   (B)   Yes, her action resulted in Flo's death.

   (C)   No, Flo's own action caused her death.

   (D)   No, the negligence of the nurses in not checking Flo more likely caused her death.

[A] Self Defense

While riding a commuter train home late one night, Bonny saw a stranger staring at her. Bonny is a petite woman (5'2" and 100 lbs). The stranger was a very large man (6'5" and 250 lbs.) with a grizzled beard and dirty, rumpled clothing. As Bonny got off the train, she noticed the man stepping out the other door. He followed her out of the train station and into the parking lot. He was walking rapidly towards her as she fumbled with her keys and started to open her car door. As he approached her car's back bumper, he reached into his pocket and muttered something unintelligible in a menacing tone. Bonnie reached under the seat of her car, pulled out a small handgun, and shot the man.

114.   Should the court allow a jury instruction on self-defense?

(A)   No, because the man did not take any specific aggressive actions toward Bonnie.

(B)   No, because Bonnie was at her car and had a duty to retreat.

(C)   Yes, because the man was bigger than Bonnie and was acting in a threatening manner.

(D)   Yes, because Bonnie truly believed that she was in imminent danger.

115.   What if the police find that the stranger was returning from a two-week hiking and backpacking trip, was reaching into his pocket for his keys because his car was right next to Bonnie's car, and was muttering under his breath because he was exhausted from his long trip? Would these facts change the result?

ANSWER:

116.   Assume that instead of shooting the hiker, Bonny pulled a knife on him. Would the stranger then be justified if he responded by shooting Bonny?

(A)   No, because one cannot use deadly force in self-defense.

(B)   No, because the response would not be proportional.

(C)   Yes; because a knife is a deadly weapon, pulling a knife necessarily justifies the use of deadly force.

(D)   Yes, because the hiker honestly believed that he was in imminent danger and that the gun was his only means of avoiding injury.

Donald and Matthew got into a verbal argument at Donald's house. Donald could see that if the argument went on much longer, it was going to become an outright fistfight. Donald stayed where he was. Matthew then shoved Donald.

117. Would Donald be justified in using the defense of self-defense if he shoved Matthew back?

   (A) No, because a little shove is not sufficient to make Matthew an aggressor.

   (B) No, because Donald has a duty to retreat.

   (C) Yes, because Matthew was the aggressor and Donald had no duty to retreat.

   (D) Yes, because no one has to accept physical contact without responding in kind.

Two uniformed police officers improperly stopped Jen as she walked home. They asked her what she was doing. She brushed past them, remarking that she was going home. The police officers stopped her again, and told Jen that they would like to talk with her. Jen told the officers that she had not done anything wrong, and she attempted to walk away again. The officers then stepped in front of Jen. She fought them, biting, scratching, and pulling the officers' hair. Ultimately, the officers got Jen into handcuffs and into a police car.

118. Was Jen justified in her response to the officers?

   (A) No, because our system protects police officers from being endangered needlessly.

   (B) No, because Jen started the fight.

   (C) Yes, because citizens have a right to resist unlawful arrests.

   (D) Yes, because Jen was outnumbered by the two officers.

Ryan yelled some insults at Bruce. Bruce turned and shoved Ryan. The two pushed each other for a short while. Ryan then pulled a knife and Bruce received several minor cuts.

119. Can Ryan claim self-defense for his use of the knife?

   (A) No, because Ryan started the argument.

   (B) No, because Ryan escalated the altercation.

   (C) Yes, because Bruce started the fight.

   (D) Yes, because Bruce was not hurt badly.

Lola and Mel were married eight years ago. After a few years of marriage, Mel began to hit Lola when he would get drunk. As the years went by, Mel drank more often, and his rages became increasingly violent. Last year, Lola was hospitalized after Mel pushed her down a flight of stairs. A few months ago, Lola was treated for a concussion after Mel hit her with a cast-iron skillet. One day, Mel came home with a gun. He told Lola that the next time she made him mad, he would kill her. That night Mel was drinking heavily, and Lola could tell that he was going to be in a violent mood. As Mel walked upstairs, Lola pushed him over the balcony. Mel broke his neck and was killed instantly.

120.   Can Lola successfully claim self-defense in response to a murder charge?

(A)   No, because she should have retreated.

(B)   No, because she was not in imminent danger.

(C)   Yes, because, as a battered spouse, Lola knew what was going to happen.

(D)   Yes, because Mel had been "asking for it."

[B]   Defense of Others

Richard was walking to his car in a busy parking lot. He saw a man step out from behind another car and grab a child. The mother of the child began screaming, "[h]e's got my baby!" The man had no visible weapon.

121.   Would Richard be justified in attacking the man?

(A)   No, because defense of others is limited to those with special relationships.

(B)   No, because Richard does not have all of the facts.

(C)   Yes, if Richard uses a reasonable amount of force based on a solid belief that a child was being abducted.

(D)   Yes, Richard can act because the child would be justified in attacking the man.

122.   Assume, in the previous scenario, that the man was actually the child's custodial father and it was the woman who was trying to abduct the child. Would the outcome change?

(A)   No, because Richard acted upon a reasonable belief.

(B)   No, because Richard's actions were not justified under either set of circumstances.

(C)   Yes, because Richard was wrong in his assessment of the situation.

(D)   Yes, because the child would not have been justified in attacking his father.

Stephan stole a valuable fishing reel from a sporting goods shop. A plain-clothes security guard ran out of the store and tackled Stephan who was fleeing. Another customer who saw the guard tackle Stephan pulled the guard off Stephan and punched the guard, knocking him unconscious.

123.   Would the customer's actions be justified as a defense of others under the historical approach? Would they be justified under the modern rule?

ANSWER:

[C] Defense of Property

Melissa left her fancy, expensive car running in front of a store while she went inside to buy some milk. As she walked out of the store, she saw a stranger opening her car door. Melissa yelled and pulled a handgun from her purse. She told the stranger to move away from her vehicle. The stranger looked at Melissa and turned to climb into the car. Melissa shot the would-be thief.

124.   In response to a murder charge, can Melissa successfully claim defense of property?

(A)   No, because shooting someone is never justified.

(B)   No, because deadly force is not justified solely for the protection of property.

(C)   Yes, because the use of force is permitted to prevent or stop the imminent theft of property.

(D)   Yes, because the car was very expensive, the use of deadly force is warranted.

Burt and his family were lying asleep in bedrooms upstairs. Burt heard a clatter on the stairs. He grabbed a baseball bat and crept down the hallway. Burt surprised a burglar, who was coming up the stairs. Burt beat him with the bat.

125.   Were Burt's actions justified?

(A)   No, because the burglar was not clearly going to injure Burt.

(B)   No, because Burt should have attempted non-violent methods of preventing the burglary.

(C)   Yes, because the use of deadly force is permissible when the home is invaded.

(D)   Yes, because Burt could reasonably have believed that attempting to stop the burglar with non-deadly force would have put his family in danger.

[D] Duress

Henrico and his girlfriend were sitting in a car parked on the street late one night. A man stepped out of the shadows and got into the backseat of the car. He pointed a gun at Henrico's girlfriend and told Henrico to start driving. Henrico did as he was told. The stranger directed Henrico to drive through town at a dangerous speed and to go the wrong direction on several one-way streets. The driver then told Henrico to stop abruptly in front of a deserted building, at which point the stranger shot and killed Henrico's girlfriend. The man then fled from the car.

126.   Can Henrico successfully use the defense of duress for the driving offenses?

ANSWER:

127. Suppose the man did not flee. Instead, he remained in the car and then instructed Henrico to get out of the car and go into the building, where a woman was lying on the floor unconscious. The man shoved Henrico across the room and kicked a knife over. With the gun still pointed at Henrico, the man told Henrico to stab the woman. Afraid for his life, Henrico stabbed the woman. She died instantly. Will the defense of duress be successful here?

ANSWER:

Daphne told Tad, her administrative assistant, that she would fire him if he refused to "cook the books." Tad reluctantly did as instructed.

128. When the auditors found the fraudulent entries, may Tad successfully defend against a criminal fraud charge by showing that he acted under duress?

   (A) No, because the threat was imminent.

   (B) No, because duress may only be used as a defense for threats of deadly force or great bodily injury.

   (C) Yes, because Daphne's threat was credible and she had the ability to carry it out.

   (D) Yes, because Tad was not at fault for being put in the threatening situation.

[E]   Necessity

Gerald was camping in the mountains when a bad storm suddenly hit. Although it was extremely early in the year for a winter storm, several feet of snow accumulated. Gerald had no equipment, clothing, or provisions to survive in such severe weather. Slowly clambering through the rocky forest, Gerald came upon a cabin. He broke in and for five days he used food and clothing he found in the cabin, until the snow had melted enough for him to hike back to town.

129. May Gerald be excused from the crimes he committed by using the defense of necessity?

   (A) No, because Gerald's lack of preparation caused his predicament.

   (B) No, because necessity is only available in life and death situations, and Gerald probably would have survived without committing any crimes.

   (C) Yes, because the harm Gerald avoided (serious injury) was a lesser evil than the harm he created (trespass and theft).

   (D) Yes, because one may always do whatever is necessary to save one's own life.

The mortgage company was about to foreclose on Immanuel's house. He knew he had to make a payment immediately, but he did not have the money. Immanuel created a check on his computer with a fake bank account number and sent it to the mortgage company. A week later, Immanuel sent a legitimate check to the mortgage company to make a real payment in order to prevent the foreclosure; he then asked the company to ignore the first check. He was nevertheless prosecuted for a fraud offense. Immanuel raised the defense of necessity, arguing that he was in dire financial straits and had to prevent his home from being taken away, just for a week, until he could make the payment.

130.   Would Immanuel's use of the necessity defense be permitted?

   (A)   No, because economic need does not justify the commission of a crime.

   (B)   Yes, although Immanuel could not rely upon the defense under the modern statutes.

   (C)   Yes, because necessity is a defense based on policy, and legislators favor home ownership.

   (D)   Yes, because Immanuel corrected his actions by making the payment as soon as his financial necessity disappeared.

Charlene was incarcerated three years ago. She knew that she was guilty and she was willing to serve her time, but the prison conditions were terrible. The guards often beat the prisoners, though Charlene herself was never beaten. The septic system frequently did not work, fouling the cells. The unsanitary conditions were absolutely unbearable. One afternoon, Charlene noticed a spot by the fence where she could not be seen by the guard towers. The next morning, she slipped, unnoticed, under the fence, and escaped. Three weeks later, she was caught and was taken back to the prison.

131.   Would Charlene be excused from the crimes related to her escape on the ground of necessity?

   (A)   No, because prisoners should expect poor treatment.

   (B)   No, because Charlene had lawful options available to her.

   (C)   Yes, because any person, including a prisoner, has a right to preserve her own life and health.

   (D)   Yes, because the danger to Charlene's life was imminent.

[F] Prevention of Crime

Some of the neighborhood kids offered to pay Carl $100 if he would break into the Jones's house and steal their new big screen television. On the appointed night, Carl broke into the house and carried the TV out onto the lawn. A police officer on patrol saw Carl. Getting out of her car, the officer yelled at Carl to stop, but Carl kept trudging toward the curb. Again, the officer yelled, warning Carl to stop or she would shoot. Frightened, Carl dropped the TV and ran. The officer shot Carl before he got very far.

132.   Does the officer have a defense of "crime prevention" (or "law enforcement") in response to a criminal charge?

(A) No, because police officers may not use deadly force in effectuating an arrest.

(B) No, because Carl was fleeing and appeared unarmed.

(C) Yes, because Carl just committed a felony.

(D) Yes, because the officer knew that Carl would get away if she did not use force to stop him.

Undercover police officer Darryl, on a coffee break, overheard some women at the 7-11 recounting their exploits from the previous night when they robbed the corner store and about what an adrenaline rush it was. He then heard the women say they were now going to rob the 7-11. Thinking that he must have misunderstood, but curious, Darryl lingered. Darryl then saw that one woman was walking around with her hand in her jacket pocket. It looked to Darryl as if she had a gun. Darryl ran down the aisle and tackled the woman.

133. May Darryl use the defense of crime prevention against a charge of battery?

(A) No, the force used was too extreme.

(B) No, because force may only be used to make an arrest after the completion of a crime, not to prevent a crime.

(C) Yes, because Darryl had reason to fear for his safety.

(D) Yes, because use of moderate force is permissible to prevent crimes.

[G] Entrapment

Known drug dealer Leon asked Cynthia if she was interested in making "some good money" because he could "hook her up with some fine stuff." Cynthia told Leon that she just got out of prison a month before for a drug offense, and she did not want to get mixed up with that kind of business again. A few months later, Leon heard that Cynthia desperately needed money. He again asked Cynthia if she would like to make some money. When Cynthia hesitated, Leon described how easy it would be, how much money she would make, and how safe it would be. Leon assured Cynthia that he had clients with whom he could connect her so that she need not risk getting caught in an undercover drug bust. Finally, after several more meetings and much coaxing, Cynthia said that she would help sell the drugs, but only until she got back on her feet. Leon was actually an undercover drug agent who had Cynthia arrested when she tried to make her first sell from the drugs Leon had provided.

134. Under the majority subjective test would Cynthia have a successful defense of entrapment?

(A) Yes, because the government supplied the drugs.

(B) No, because Cynthia willingly committed the crime.

(C) No, because Leon's actions were not overly coercive.

(D) Yes, because Cynthia was not predisposed to commit the crime when Leon first contacted her.

135. Under the objective test (used by some states and adopted in the Model Penal Code), would Cynthia have a successful defense of entrapment?

    (A) No, because Cynthia willingly agreed to deal drugs.

    (B) No, because Cynthia was predisposed to deal drugs.

    (C) Yes, because Leon's persistent actions induced Cynthia into criminal activity.

    (D) Yes, because Cynthia gave up drug dealing earlier.

Renée had four prior convictions for prostitution, the most recent being five years ago. Late one night, as she was walking down the street on her way home from a club, a car pulled up next to her. The man offered her twice what she used to make for a sexual act. Renée adamantly declined. As she continued walking down the street, the man drove alongside her and doubled his offer, making it four times the amount customers normally paid for such acts. Renée hesitated, but decided that she could not afford to pass up so much money and agreed to perform the illegal act. The man turned out to be an undercover police officer and had her arrested.

136. Does Renée have a successful defense of entrapment, using the subjective test?

    (A) No, because Renée was predisposed to engage in prostitution.

    (B) No, because Renée performed the illegal act for the money.

    (C) Yes, because the police officer offered an irresistible amount of money.

    (D) Yes, because Renée appears to have given up prostitution years before, and seemed reluctant at the start.

A sting operation was created to catch high school students suspected of selling marijuana to middle school students. Fernando was a high school student who had been arrested for selling drugs. In exchange for Fernando's assistance, the prosecutor agreed to drop the pending drug charges against him. Acting as an undercover agent, Fernando asked students who had sold drugs in the past to sell marijuana again. They readily agreed and Fernando gave them marijuana provided to him by the police. Once arrested for selling the marijuana, the students claimed that they were entrapped.

137. Will their defense be successful under the subjective test of entrapment?

    (A) No, because the students were already drug dealers and were not reluctant to continue selling drugs.

    (B) No, because Fernando was not a police officer.

    (C) Yes, because they were selling drugs provided by the police.

    (D) Yes, because they would not have agreed to sell the drugs if they had known that Fernando was working for the police.

Two tests are used in the United States to determine whether a defendant has been entrapped. The majority, subjective test is based on the "predisposition" of the defendant to commit the crime. The objective test considers the behavior of a reasonable person in response to the actions of the government. A number of states (California, Michigan, Iowa, Texas, et al.) have adopted the objective test.

138. Which of the following considerations forms the primary basis for the objective test?

   (A) People who are culpable should be held accountable.

   (B) The judicial branch should provide a check against the executive branch.

   (C) Looking to the culpability of the individual defendant, courts can evaluate whether that person would have committed a crime without government inducement.

   (D) The police need a wide range of options in the efforts to reduce crime.

For a long time, marijuana had grown in Wayne's field. Earlier this year, Wayne was convicted of marijuana possession. Wayne harvested the field twice in the last five years, selling the hemp for clothing production. He also had other brushes with the law. Three years ago, Wayne was convicted of selling marijuana. Recently, law enforcement officials made a deal with Dustin, a drug dealer, to buy a large quantity of marijuana from Wayne. Dustin placed the order and paid for the shipment with money provided by the government. After selling the marijuana, Wayne was arrested. He claimed that he was entrapped.

139. Under the majority view, which piece of evidence may the government introduce to show that Wayne was not entrapped?

   (A) Wayne had marijuana growing in his field.

   (B) Wayne was previously convicted of possession of marijuana.

   (C) Wayne was previously convicted of selling marijuana.

   (D) All of the above.

Rosaline is an expert shot with a rifle. After being released from prison for murder, an undercover police officer approached her about killing a "competing drug dealer." After several meetings to work out the details, the officer made the payment. Rosaline went to the top of a building with a high-powered rifle. She had her target in sight and had just pulled the trigger when a police officer arrested her. Although Rosaline hit her target, the dealer was not killed. Rosaline argued that she was entrapped.

140. Under either of the two tests, was she entrapped?

   (A) No, because a defense of entrapment is not available for attempted murder.

   (B) No, because Rosaline did not complete the crime that the officer had paid her to do.

   (C) Yes, because the police exceeded the bounds of propriety in hiring her to kill a person.

   (D) Yes, because she would never have committed murder without the officer's inducement.

Duane's drug lab was shut down after the police arrested his chemist on other charges. Noah, an undercover officer, agreed to help Duane get the illegal lab running again. Soon, they were actively producing large quantities of drugs. Once the business was running and Noah was involved in it, Duane then recruited Farah to help with packaging and distribution. Both Duane and Farah were later arrested for manufacturing and distributing drugs. Both argued that they were entrapped.

141.   Assuming that Duane is acquitted of the charges after the jury accepted his defense of entrapment resulting from police over-involvement, could the jury also find that Farah was entrapped?

(A)   No, because Duane was not a government agent.

(B)   No, because Farah was willing to participate.

(C)   Yes, because all third parties are accorded the entrapment defense if the primary defendant is successful in raising the issue.

(D)   Yes, because the entire business would not have existed, but for the government's participation.

Louis was a smuggler. He claimed that he could get anything into the country from Asia. An undercover officer asked Louis to smuggle rare antiques. Louis knew it was illegal to import such items. Louis agreed and delivered the antiques.

142.   Was Louis entrapped according to the majority test?
ANSWER:

143.   Was Louis entrapped according to the minority test?

[H]   Intoxication

Mark had a severe drinking problem that caused him to miss work frequently. When Mark was fired for his absences, he headed straight from work to a bar for a drink. As the day progressed, he became more and more inebriated and the bartender finally refused to serve him any more drinks. Mark then bought a bottle of vodka and continued drinking at home. After nine hours of drinking, Mark could barely stand. He called his ex-girlfriend, Tara, at her apartment. When a male voice answered the phone, Mark hung up. The thought of his ex in a new relationship enraged him. Mark took a cab to her apartment. When he arrived, a man answered the door. Before the man could say anything, Mark attacked him. The two men ended up on the third floor landing. After several minutes of struggling, Mark pushed the other man away. The man fell backward down a set of concrete stairs and smashed his skull. The man died several days later. The next day, Mark barely remembered the previous day, although he vaguely recalled fighting with someone. Mark's ex-girlfriend, who watched the scene from inside of her apartment, relayed the details of the fight to the authorities.

144.   Under the majority rule, can Mark claim his intoxication as a defense to murder?

(A) No, because a defendant's intoxication can never be introduced as evidence for the defense.

(B) No, because there is no complete defense of intoxication.

(C) Yes, because Mark is an alcoholic and it is unconstitutional to punish someone for such a disease.

(D) Yes, because Mark's intoxication prevented him from having the capacity to form the intent to murder.

145. In the previous problem, on what grounds could evidence of voluntary intoxication allow Mark to escape all criminal liability for the killing?

ANSWER:

In a prosecution in which the defendant is charged with attempted murder, the defendant offered evidence of extreme intoxication at the time of the crime.

146. What would be an appropriate instruction to the jury?

(A) If you find that the defendant killed the victim, but she was too inebriated to be fairly held for her actions, you must find her not guilty.

(B) If you find that the defendant killed the victim, you may not consider any evidence of her intoxicated condition because intoxication is not a defense.

(C) If you find, based upon the totality of the evidence, that the government did not demonstrate that the defendant intended to kill, then you must find the defendant not guilty.

(D) You must find that the defendant intended to kill in order to return a guilty verdict. You may not consider, on this issue, her level of intoxication.

Brandi was invited to a party at the home of her friend Luis. When she arrived, Luis encouraged her to drink some punch. Brandi declined, telling him that she was "trying to cut down on the liquor I drink." In response, Luis said, "No problem, there's no alcohol in the punch." Brandi then drank several large glasses of the punch. Unbeknownst to both Brandi and Luis, another guest had secretly "spiked" the punch by putting in a large amount of a potent drug. The drug caused Brandi to go berserk, yell at Luis, and then slug him in the face with a large wooden bowl. Luis died soon thereafter from the blow to the head. Brandi is charged with murder.

147. Can she claim involuntary intoxication as a defense?

(A) Yes, because her intoxication was truly involuntary. As she did not intend to take any drug, she could not have foreseen the effects.

(B) No, it is common knowledge that all sorts of ingredients go into punch. For this reason, Brandi accepted that risk when she drank the punch, so her intoxication was not involuntary.

(C)   No, because involuntary intoxication is not a defense to a violent criminal charge.

(D)   No, because Brandi voluntarily became intoxicated when she drank large amounts of the punch.

148.   Would the result change if—before drinking the punch—another guest had said to Brandi: "I wouldn't drink that stuff, I hear it's been spiked with something weird."?

ANSWER:

[I]   Insanity Defense

At his trial for first-degree murder in the killing of his girlfriend, Jeff claimed that he heard voices from God at the time, directing Jeff to kill his girlfriend to prevent the world from coming to an end. While he did not want to kill her and knew that it would be illegal, Jeff believed the voices in his head and thought that Armageddon would result if he did not kill her. Jeff raised the insanity defense. The defense expert testified that Jeff attempted to get psychiatric help in the past for his condition, but that all of the doctors had failed in their treatment. This doctor further testified that Jeff's condition could be remedied by a regimen of anti-psychotic drugs. In fact, by the time of the trial, such a program had already succeeded in restoring Jeff to a nearly normal condition. Since Jeff had been seeing this particular doctor, he no longer suffered from the extreme hallucinations and uncontrollably violent rampages that destroyed his professional and personal life up until the time he killed his girlfriend.

149.   Which of the following would be the most appropriate jury instruction in a majority of jurisdictions?

(A)   If the killing was the product of a mental disease, you must find the defendant not guilty.

(B)   If the defendant did not know the difference between right and wrong at the time of the killing and if the killing was a result of mental impairment, you must find the defendant not guilty.

(C)   If the defendant could not control his impulse to kill even though he was aware it was wrong, you must find the defendant not guilty.

(D)   If the defendant, as a result of a mental disease or defect, lacked the substantial capacity to appreciate the wrongfulness of his conduct or to conform his conduct to the law, you must find the defendant not guilty.

150.   Assume that Jeff's case is tried in a jurisdiction that adheres to the *M'Naughten* test of insanity. Can the judge exclude evidence that Jeff heard voices instructing him to kill?

ANSWER:

151. Could the judge in Jeff's case also exclude testimony from a defense expert that "Jeff suffered from a mental illness which caused him to kill his girlfriend"?

    (A) Yes, because experts are not allowed to testify to the ultimate issue of insanity.

    (B) Yes, because such evidence is irrelevant to a case under the *M'Naughten* rule.

    (C) No, because the jury is entitled to hear all evidence which pertains to a defendant's mental capacity at the time of the killing in order to make an informed decision.

    (D) No, because a qualified expert is allowed to present his professional opinion to the jury.

152. TRUE OR FALSE: In a majority of states, the burden of proof as to the insanity defense is on the defendant? Explain.

ANSWER:

Assume that Jeff has decided not to present an insanity defense at trial. He and his attorney concluded that the government will likely not be able to prove all the elements of the murder charge. Moreover, even if the government were to win the case, Jeff does not want to be sent to a mental institution, a consequence of a successful insanity defense in his state. At trial, the defense introduced some evidence about Jeff's unstable and confused mental state for the past several years, hoping the jury would conclude that Jeff could not have formed the necessary intent to kill. One of Jeff's friends described several instances in which she found Jeff sitting in a room alone responding to voices that he seemed to be hearing. This testimony concerned the trial judge who believed that Jeff was severely disturbed and deserved to get psychiatric treatment in a hospital, not a lifetime in the prison system. The judge raised the insanity defense over Jeff's objections and instructed the jury accordingly.

153. Was this action erroneous?

    (A) No, because the judge has discretion to raise the defense if it seems that Jeff could be found insane.

    (B) No, because the judge is obligated to raise the defense if it seems that Jeff could be found insane.

    (C) Yes, the judge's action deprived the defendant of the ability to strategize about his defense with his attorney.

    (D) Yes, because it is very unlikely that a jury would find Jeff not guilty based on the insanity defense.

[J] Diminished Capacity

Deborah was on trial for the first-degree murder of her toddler. She claimed that she had mental problems, and as a result she did not remember the killing and had no memory of the entire evening at issue. In addition, the defendant called both Deborah's therapist and many family members to testify that Deborah was having severe psychological problems at the time of the killing. These people testified that Deborah was unstable, forgot basic daily tasks, acted inappropriately in public, and demonstrated the effects of serious mental illness on occasion. The defendant carefully did not offer an insanity defense. The government objected to the defendant offering any testimony about her psychiatric condition.

154. Should the defendant have been allowed to offer such evidence?

   (A) No, at least as to the non-experts, Deborah's family members were unqualified to speak to this question.

   (B) No, because such testimony is irrelevant if Deborah is not offering the insanity defense.

   (C) Yes, because all the evidence would relate to the state of mind requirement and is therefore relevant in disproving the murder charge.

   (D) Yes, because the jury could find the defendant insane even if the insanity defense has not been raised.

155. In the previous case, what would be an appropriate instruction on this evidence?
ANSWER:

[K] Competency to Stand Trial

Since Danilo's arrest, his mental condition has deteriorated considerably. He no longer responds to questioning and he insists that his dead mother is still alive. His doctor's evaluation concludes that he has delusions that cause him to lapse between reality and illusion.

156. Should Danilo's lawyer raise this matter pre-trial?

   (A) No, this information would be relevant at trial in disproving the ability to form the state of mind required of the crime.

   (B) No, this information would be helpful at trial in offering an excuse for the committed crime.

   (C) Yes, the lawyer should raise the matter before trial in connection with an insanity defense.

   (D) Yes, the lawyer should raise the issue of competency to stand trial in light of this evidence.

PRACTICE FINAL EXAM

QUESTIONS

Angie became very drunk while out with her boyfriend and some other friends at a pool hall. The couple had been having difficulties for some time, and the two of them often argued. Very late that evening, Angie got a ride home from Mike, a friend of her boyfriend. Her boyfriend appeared at her apartment an hour or so later, claiming that she had been unfaithful to him when she left the pool hall early with Mike. He then slapped her once. She yelled, "I wish you would just die!" and pushed him down the stairs to the basement. He died after hitting his head on the steps.

157. If the government demonstrates she intended to kill him, and Angie offers no defense to the charge, of what crime will she most likely be convicted?

    (A) First degree murder.

    (B) Voluntary manslaughter.

    (C) Negligent homicide.

    (D) Nothing, because she was intoxicated.

Tom was on a long trip and decided to pick up a hitchhiker on the side of the highway. The stranger looked a little odd but seemed nice enough, and the two traveled for an hour or so together. Tom then said he needed to get some gas. Bart, the hitchhiker, told Tom he planned to "hit up the place" so he could get some cash. Bart showed Tom his loaded pistol and jokingly said that Tom could consider the free gas his contribution for the ride. Tom said nothing about the proposed crime but pulled into the nearest station. After Tom gassed up his car, while Bart was in the store, Tom jumped in his car and drove off to the highway. He never reported anything to anyone. After robbing the station, Bart was apprehended and told the police of his conversation with Tom.

158. Can Tom be found guilty of conspiracy to commit armed robbery?

    (A) No, because he never agreed to commit the crime and he may have been acting under duress.

    (B) No, because Tom withdrew from the plan, providing him an affirmative defense.

    (C) Yes, because Tom helped Bart by bringing him to the right place, by following his instructions, and by not reporting the crime immediately.

    (D) Yes, because an agreement to rob the store can be inferred from the actions of the pair.

159. What if Tom and Bart actually knew each other from years previous? Say, for example, that they were cellmates in a county jail some time ago and they also had similar convictions for theft and armed robbery. Would this change the result?

ANSWER:

Kim and Matt concocted a plan to kidnap college student Tamara and not release her until her parents paid them $1 million. The two agreed that no weapons were to be used at any time and the woman was not to be harmed in any way. Matt was supposed to wait by Tamara's college dormitory and lure her to a van by asking for her help carrying some packages. Tamara was suspicious, but Matt managed to get her in the van. As they were driving out of the city to a mountain cabin to hide out, a tractor-trailer slammed into them. The accident was not Matt's fault, but Tamara died several days later of her injuries.

160. Can Matt be convicted of murder?

(A) Yes, because he intended to kidnap her, he can be found guilty of felony murder.

(B) Yes, because he intended for her to die.

(C) No, because he did not intend for her to die.

(D) No, because he did not intend for her to be hurt and the accident was unforeseeable.

Suppose, in the previous problem, that Tamara did not get into the van willingly. Matt then pulled out a weapon and threatened her. They struggled, and the gun went off, killing Tamara. Kim, who was waiting in the driver's seat, had no idea that Matt had a gun.

161. Can Kim, nonetheless, be convicted of murder?

(A) Yes, because she would be responsible for Tamara's death, even if the death was unforeseeable.

(B) Yes, because she was a co-conspirator in the kidnapping and therefore can be found responsible for the actions of her co-conspirator and the consequences of that conspiracy.

(C) No, because the killing was accidental.

(D) No, because unlike Matt, Kim had nothing to do with Tamara's death. They had agreed that no weapons of any kind would be used.

Jennifer was found guilty of conspiring to commit armed robbery. She and a former roommate had planned, with another acquaintance, to rob a local bank. According to the testimony of the arresting officers and the other co-conspirators, Jennifer exhibited signs of mental illness: she often had conversations with imaginary people, she sometimes acted and dressed in combat gear in preparation for "the coming invasion," and she had a history of treatment in mental health facilities. A few key rulings from the trial are being offered at the appellate level. Although defense counsel never raised the insanity defense at trial, at one point during the defense presentation, the defense lawyers elicited the testimony of Dr. Sissy, a renowned mental health expert. At the conclusion of the trial, the judge provided instruction as to the insanity defense even though counsel objected to the instruction.

162. Was the evidence of mental illness irrelevant if defense counsel did not put forth the insanity defense at trial?

(A) Yes, because the mental condition of the defendant should have no bearing on the outcome unless the insanity defense is presented.

(B) Yes, because the mental illness of the defendant does not matter in a conspiracy case.

(C) No, because counsel may have been arguing that the government failed to prove its case.

(D) No, because the evidence so clearly demonstrated that the defendant did not know right from wrong.

163. In the previous question, was the trial judge's instruction correctly given?

(A) No, because his instruction violated Jennifer's right to decide the manner in which defenses were raised at trial.

(B) No, because Jennifer could very well be insane and therefore incompetent to stand trial.

(C) Yes, because the judge must ensure the defendant gets an entirely fair trial and an insanity instruction could only help the defendant.

(D) Yes, the judge has the ultimate duty to ensure that the defendant receives a fair trial.

The expert testimony has also raised an appellate issue in Jennifer's trial. On cross-examination, the prosecution asked two questions of its expert witness. First, "Dr. Phil, does Jennifer suffer from a mental illness?" Second, "On the day in question, could Jennifer—as a result of her mental illness—understand the difference between right and wrong?" Over the objection of the defense, the judge allowed Dr. Phil to answer both questions. To the first question, he stated, "Yes, I think she does have a mental illness." To the second, Dr. Phil said, "It is so difficult for me to say with any certainty, but I suppose I think she probably could understand the difference between right and wrong."

164. Should these questions and answers have been allowed?
ANSWER:

Walt owned a general store next to a high school. From the hours of 2:00 p.m. to 4:00 p.m., he generally sold a large quantity of potent household cleaners, mostly to kids stopping by on their way home from school. At times, it seemed odd to him that he sold so many of these kinds of products, considering the nature of his store and the fact that his teenage son never helped out with the housework. He asked his son about this and the boy said that lots of teens were into "huffing" cleaning solvents. Wanting to preserve the profits of the store in any way he could, Walt expanded the selection and the number of cleaning products he sold. Shortly after, a teenager who routinely bought cleaning products from Walt was found dead as a result of inhaling the fumes from a cleaning solvent. The particular product causing the death was known to have been purchased two days earlier from Walt's store.

165.   Could Walt be found guilty of a homicide offense?
ANSWER:

Betty is a private nurse who worked and lived in Martin's household. Betty was the only member of the household staff who saw widower Martin on a regular basis. Martin's doctor advised complete bed rest and quiet, and warned that with his deadly heart condition any other lifestyle would hasten his death. Betty grew to dislike Martin intensely. One day, Betty was in the house when Martin hit the "panic button" beside his bed. This button was only to be used when he needed emergency medical attention. Hearing the buzzer, Betty remembered she did not give Martin his heart medicine that morning. Nevertheless, she decided to finish folding the linens before she went to look in on him. An hour later, when she checked on him, Betty found Martin dead.

166.   Can Betty be found guilty of a homicide offense?

(A)   Yes, because she committed actions that led to his death. By failing to give the medication and then delaying her response to the "panic button," she engaged in grossly reckless behavior.

(B)   Yes, but the only conviction could be on a charge of negligent homicide.

(C)   No, because in most states the criminal law does not impose a duty to act to help someone in need.

(D)   No, because Betty did not cause Martin's death.

Dirk and Eric were opposed to the federal government's foreign policies. The Secretary of State came to their town to give a speech to community leaders, and Dirk and Eric decided to join in a protest demonstration. They arrived at the meeting hall and linked up with several groups opposing the administration's foreign policy. When the group of government cars, including the Secretary of State's, arrived at the meeting hall, Dirk and Eric threw rice at the cars and yelled, "Send Food Not Bombs!" When the Secretary was walking into the building, they used very powerful bullhorns and screamed at him, calling him a murderer and a criminal. Dirk and Eric were quickly arrested for violating a state law that provides the following:

"A person is guilty of disorderly conduct when in a public place, and with intent to cause public inconvenience, annoyance or alarm, he or she makes an unreasonable noise."

167. What challenges will Dirk and Eric raise at their trial for violating the law?
ANSWER:

Mark and Pedro were cellmates several years ago in the state prison. They had both been convicted of drug distribution and both were heroin addicts themselves. When Mark was released, he went through a job training program, found a small apartment, and generally pulled his life together. A year later, Pedro was let out of prison as well. They ran into each other and spent a few hours catching up. Pedro was looking for a place to live, and Mark suggested Pedro move into his building. Thereafter, they saw each other often. Pedro did not last long before returning to his old ways, using and selling drugs. Over an eight-month period, Pedro continuously offered Mark drugs, and Mark continuously, and angrily, refused. Then Mark lost his job and could not find another one. His previous conviction kept standing in his way. Pedro came over for a visit and again offered Mark something to "help him with his troubles." Mark accepted and began using illegal narcotics. During this time, Pedro was working as a government informant. A week later, Mark's apartment was searched, drugs were found, and he was arrested and charged with possession of heroin again. Mark's lawyer is raising the entrapment defense.

168. Will the defense likely be successful?

(A) Yes, because Mark was so reluctant.

(B) Yes, because the government conduct violated Due Process.

(C) No, because Pete was not an actual government officer, just an informant.

(D) No, because Mark would have returned to drugs even without Pete's influence.

Officer Knight was dispatched to a residence after a 911 call reporting a suspicious man leaving a neighbor's house. As he pulled into the driveway of the home, Knight spotted Tom running through a neighboring field. Officer Knight gave chase on foot, and yelled, "Stop, police!" Tom kept running, pulling away from the officer. The officer threatened, "Stop, or I'll shoot!" but Tom continued to flee. Officer Knight shot Tom in the back, and Tom died immediately. A later investigation showed that Tom was unarmed, but he had just burglarized a house.

169. In response to a criminal charge, does the officer have a valid defense?

(A) No, because under the fleeing felon doctrine, the suspect needs to have been attempting to commit, or fleeing from, a felony.

(B) No, because Tom did not pose a serious and immediate danger to the officer or to others, Officer Knight had no justification for shooting at him.

(C) Yes, under the fleeing felon doctrine, if the officer had a reasonable belief that the suspect was a fleeing felon, then the actions can be justified.

(D) Yes, under the fleeing felon doctrine, the officer is not justified in killing a suspect, only in wounding him to prevent further flight.

Bertha and Adam were college sweethearts. They were crushed to learn that Bertha was pregnant. They believed, however, that they could cope with the birth of the child. They were wrong. The child was delivered at a secluded farmhouse by Adam who had read up on child delivery procedures. Immediately after the delivery, Adam handed the child to Bertha. She looked at the child, looked at Adam and said, "We can't keep this child." Adam took the child, brought it to the barn and suffocated it with a towel. Medical testimony at the murder trial of Adam will indicate the child lived for less than five minutes.

170.   Will this testimony defeat the murder prosecution?

    (A)   Yes, it was not clear at that point that the child would have survived even with proper attention.

    (B)   Yes, Adam was under no duty to assist the child.

    (C)   No, even five minutes of life is sufficient to show that a homicide took place.

    (D)   No, Adam would have been guilty even if the child had not survived the birth process.

Jeremy is on trial for the crime of rape. He claims that he had sexual intercourse with the victim, but that it was consensual. His lawyer advised him against accepting a plea bargain offered by the government because, the lawyer said, Jeremy has a very strong case. This view is based on the defense team investigations, which turned up a witness who can testify that, a year previous, he had sex with the victim. In addition, the victim's "open" lifestyle might lead the jury to conclude that the encounter was consensual.

171.   Is the advice of Jeremy's attorney sound?

    (A)   Yes, because lack of consent is not an element of a sexual assault charge.

    (B)   Yes, because the previous sexual encounter would be strong evidence for the defendant.

    (C)   No, because even if the defense lawyer demonstrates the victim had previously had consensual sex with others, it does not prove that she had consensual sex on the occasion in question.

    (D)   No, because the defense attorney will likely be barred from offering this evidence.

Stella wanted to kill her boss, as she told several of her friends. One day she became angry with the boss, screamed at him and said, "I just wish you would die today." After work that day, she purchased a large hunting knife at a sporting goods store, figured out on an internet direction line how to drive to the boss' home, and called the boss's wife to find out what time he would be returning. The wife, suspicious, phoned the police who were able to trace the call to Stella. Officers immediately arrested her.

172.   On this evidence, can Stella be convicted of attempted murder?

    (A)   Yes, her intent to kill is certain.

(B)   Yes, she took a number of steps on the road to a murder.

(C)   No, her steps were merely acts of preparation in nature.

(D)   No, it would not be attempted murder until she pulled the knife on the boss.

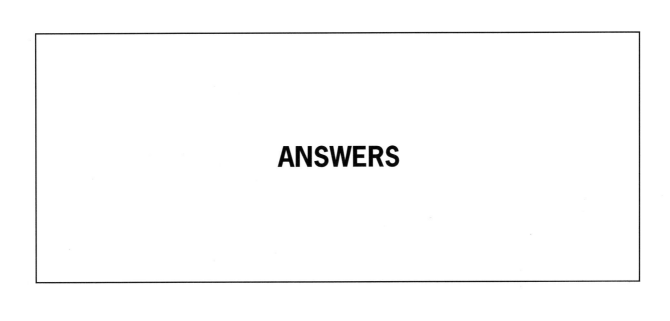

ANSWERS

1. **The correct answer is C.** The Supreme Court held, in *Robinson v. California*, 370 U.S. 660 (1962), that it would violate the Constitution for the government to make illegal a status or disease such as narcotics addiction. In terms of the way in which the prosecution might nevertheless prove such a case, **answer A is incorrect** because it is not at all clear that the officer's observation alone would be sufficient evidence upon which to convict. The standard is whether reasonable jurors could find sufficient evidence to conclude, beyond a reasonable doubt, that the government has proved each element of the crime. *Dickerson v. City of Richmond*, 346 S.E. 2d 333 (Va. App. 1986).

   While the officer's observation, taken with Charlie's statement, could well be enough to convict, **answer B is incorrect** because the statute would be found to be invalid for constitutional grounds, as noted above. **Answer D is incorrect, too.** Apart from other problems with the prosecution here, Charlie's statement would otherwise be admissible against him. Under the facts here, the statement would not raise serious questions under either the 4th Amendment (unreasonable searches and seizures) or the 5th Amendment (privilege against self-incrimination). Because Charlie's statement would fall within a recognized exception to the hearsay rule, it also would not raise a serious question under the rules of evidence.

2. Yes. While Charlie could not be convicted of a crime directly related to his disease or status, as indicated above, the rule is quite different regarding acts committed, even acts committed in furtherance of his status. Thus, if Charlie was charged with burglary and he could show that he stole in order to support his need for illegal narcotics, the trial court would reject such evidence. The Supreme Court in *Robinson* held that the actions of an addicted person are subject to criminal sanctions, even though the status of that same person would not be similarly subjected. Appearing in public while under the influence falls within the scope of actions taken, and is not mere punishment for an addict's status, hence a conviction would be allowed.

3. **The best answer is A.** It is true that the Supreme Court held that an addict could be punished for committing crimes in furtherance of his habit, *Robinson*. However, in *Powell v. Texas*, 392 U.S. 514 (1968), a majority of the Court found that punishing someone for being drunk in public would violate the Constitution if the person could show that he had nowhere else to go. If Charlie could demonstrate his addiction and his lack of private space in which to drink, his conviction would fail.

   Answer B is not the best answer because it fails to address the issue of whether Charlie's presence in public is based upon his voluntary choice to leave his home while under the influence. In this case, because Charlie had nowhere else to go, he may successfully argue that his arrest amounted to an impermissible prosecution based on his status as an addict in a way that a person who had other alternatives would not be charged. Thus, **answer D is wrong**. **Answer C is not correct.** While answer C presents another possible constitutional bar to criminal statutes, it is not operative here. Citizens must be given fair notice of laws which prohibit behavior. Publication constitutes fair notice. Because the statute in question gave proper notice here, Charlie could not successfully argue that he lacked knowledge of the illegality of his conduct.

4. Yes. If a statute is not properly defined, in such a way that the average person could not understand its meaning, a court may declare the law void for vagueness, invalid under the Due Process Clause. *Kolender v. Lawson*, 461 U.S. 352 (1983). This result stems from the guarantee of due process, which prohibits punishing a person for violating a law that is generally unintelligible. Because judges recognize the difficulty legislators face in crafting criminal codes that adequately anticipate future conduct, the courts are reluctant to strictly invoke this doctrine. For this reason, even laws that an experienced lawyer would have a difficult time comprehending are often upheld despite vagueness challenges. Moreover, even absent a statutory definition for the phrase "reckless driving," if courts in the jurisdiction (or even other jurisdictions) have interpreted its meaning, or if the phrase has roots in common law jurisprudence, the statute will likely survive a vagueness challenge. Here, the phrase "reckless driving" has been invoked, applied, and interpreted repeatedly to include conduct such as Jo's. Thus, despite the law's apparent lack of clarity, Jo's challenge will likely fail.

[A] The Act

[1] Failure to Act

5. **The correct answer is D.** Generally, the criminal law imposes no duty to act to help others. This general rule remains true even in situations in which a failure to act seems morally reprehensible. The law remains clear in refusing to impose an obligation to act. *State v. Ulvinen*, 313 N.W.2d 425 (Minn. 1981). Hence **answers A and B are incorrect.** The "no duty" rule applies even to those with great skills or expertise, so **answer C is incorrect.**

6. Yes, Erin would now likely be found guilty of a serious homicide offense. While individuals normally do not owe any duty of assistance to strangers, there will be such a duty in limited situations, such as with a family relationship (*see* question 8.) A contractual relationship, if breached, can also give rise to a criminal standard of care. Erin agreed, as part of her employment situation, to assist accident victims either by providing aid or advising others to do so. By not fulfilling her obligation, she has caused great harm and will be found criminally responsible. *Commonwealth v. Pestinikas*, 617 A.2d 1339 (Pa. 1992).

7. **The best answer is B,** as most states have hit-and-run statutes, which require those involved in a serious accident, even those who are not at fault in causing the accident, to either render assistance or report the incident. Alaska Stat. 28.35.060; Cal. Veh. Code 20003. Thus, **answer D is incorrect.** While Troy is obliged to act here, it is because of a statutory duty, not a moral duty, so **answer A is wrong.** **Answer C is incorrect** because the statutory mandate concerning those involved in serious accidents is an explicit exception to the generally accepted rule of no duty to others.

8. **The correct answer is A.** When the victims of crimes are children, many jurisdictions impose special responsibilities to act on their behalf. *Jones v. United States*, 308 F.2d 307 (D.C. Cir. 1962). Certainly in this case, Matthew owes his children that special responsibility as he is their father and was in a unique position to discover and prevent the crime of abuse. **Answer B is incorrect** as Matthew, the young girl's father, would be responsible for the abuse even if he did not pose a specific question to his daughter. Because Matthew is her father, he is expected to be involved in her life and take actions to ensure that she is safe. For this reason, **answer C is also incorrect. Answer D** is certainly true insofar as Matthew's wife is primarily responsible for the abuse. However, this does not answer the question as to Matthew's culpability, which exists apart from his wife's liability. Thus, **answer D is incorrect.**

9. No, for Marianna had not taken any steps in furtherance of her plan. The law punishes culpable intent together with actions, but the criminal law does not punish mere thoughts. *United States v. Candoli*, 870 F.2d 496 (9th Cir. 1989). The criminal law's act requirement stems partly from practical reasons; we cannot be sure of another person's thoughts if no action has been taken upon them. Moreover, the act requirement recognizes that people may think horrible thoughts, including wishes to seriously harm others, but that many of these people will never act upon their thoughts. In this case, even if Marianna fully intended to carry out her plan, she might not have gone through with it. Therefore, no criminal charge can be maintained against her.

[2] The Voluntary Act

10. **The best answer is A.** The law can only punish those who act consciously and voluntarily. *State v. Hinkle*, 489 S.E. 2d 257 (1996). Because the cause of the accident was the unknown brain disorder, Betty will not be found guilty of any crime. **Answer C, then, is wrong.** While offering to drive her friends was a conscious and voluntary act, the specific cause of the accident was her disorder, not her offer, so **answer D is also wrong. Answer B does not apply to this situation**. Once the offer of the ride was made, Betty would be responsible generally for her friends, though not here where she was unaware of her medical problem.

11. Yes, Betty could now be held responsible. The chargeable criminal act here would not be unconsciously going off the road. Rather, it would be getting into the car with her friends and knowing of the substantial risk that her medical condition could result in serious dangers to all of them. Under those circumstances, her knowledge, coupled with her behavior, would make for clear culpability and criminal liability. *State v. Olsen*, 160 P. 2d 427 (Utah 1945).

12. **The best answer is C.** Courts generally imply a requirement of voluntary action even if the statute or ordinance in question does not specify such a requirement. Judges will imply such an element because of the importance of the *actus reas* requirement throughout the history of the common law. Such a mandate is thus viewed as intended by the legislature, even if not explicitly included. Here, it seems likely that a court would see Morgan's drunkenness as a voluntary action, but not his decision to go into public while drunk. If the officers' conduct appears to be intended to lure him into public space in order to arrest him for the crime, the defense will have a winning voluntariness argument. *Martin v. State*, 17 So.2d 427 (Ala. 1944). Since the courts usually imply a voluntary act requirement, **answer A is incorrect**.

    Answer B is not correct, even though courts usually have little tolerance for excuses made for drunkenness, as shown in the later problems involving intoxication as a defense. Here, however, it does not appear that Morgan intended to venture out in public, and that he did so only under coercion by the police. A fact-finder would certainly have enough evidence to conclude that Morgan's walk to the sidewalk was involuntary, and that the act requirement implied in the statute was absent. Even though the elements of the crime might otherwise be shown, Morgan could not be convicted. For this reason, **answer D is also incorrect.**

[B] The Mental State

13. **The correct answer is C.** The required state of mind for the statute is knowledge. This is interpreted to mean that an actor can be held responsible for injuries to his child, under the statute, if he was subjectively aware that his child was at risk. *Fabritz v. Traurig*, 583 F.2d 697 (4th Cir. 1978). The prior similar episode, along with Tamika's violent temper, would likely be enough to find Rick guilty of the crime. Thus, **answer B is not correct. Answers A and D are wrong** because Rick did have the opportunity to realize the threat to his children. If, however, there were no prior incidents to create this knowledge on Rick's part, and Tamika did not have an especially violent temper, answer B would be correct. In cases such as this, Rick would be held culpable because, among other reasons, his knowledge of the situation put him in the best position to prevent the harm to his children.

14. Ignorance of the law is generally no defense, even in cases where knowledge is required in the statute. *United States v. International Minerals & Chemicals Co.*, 402 U.S. 558 (1971). Had Frieda been unaware of the gas tank, because she had borrowed the car—for instance—she could challenge the charge on the ground that she did not have the requisite mental state to be found guilty. As Frieda did know about the gasoline, she cannot make this argument. She would likely claim that the law was not intended to apply to such situations. Instead, the law was directed toward commercial carriers of dangerous chemicals, not persons such as herself who would not reasonably know about the laws governing the transportation of common chemicals. The claim would not prevail, however, because the knowledge requirement relates to the transportation and is not limited in the statute.

15. **The correct answer is D.** Drunken driving in many states is considered a strict liability crime. These crimes require no showing of a particular mental state. *Staples v. United States*, 511 U.S. 600 (1994). Strict liability crimes are generally exceptions in the criminal law because the question of culpable mental state is so central to our society's decisions, in criminal sanctions. Other than answer D, each of the other responses contends that Adam did not have the requisite state of mind to be convicted of driving while intoxicated, but many such criminal statutes have no state of mind requirement, beyond knowledge of driving after consuming alcohol. Generally, every criminal law has a specified or implied *mens rea* requirement, but in this case, no additional state of mind is required for conviction. The mere act of drinking and driving has been determined to be of such significant character that the act alone can permit culpability. Thus, **answers A, B and C are incorrect** because none of the claims would further Adam's defense.

16. **The best answer is B. Answer A is not the best answer.** Attempted murder would not likely be a successful charge against Adam. Although his actions did threaten the victim's life, he did not act with intent to harm the child. Attempt crimes always require that the defendant acted purposefully or with intent, as explained below. Part of the reason for this requirement is that attempt sentences carry fairly significant penalties. Yet the most important reason society demands such actions are taken with intent is that people who act purposefully are considered more culpable and more deserving of punishment than those whose actions mistakenly

result in harm to others. **Answer C is not correct.** The charge of manslaughter, would be a viable option, and Adam's most likely conviction, had the victim died. As the girl survived, though, this charge is unavailable to the prosecutor in this case. Manslaughter varies from the crime of murder only in the lower state of mind needed. In all cases, however, the victim must die. *United States v. LaFleur*, 971 F.2d 200 (9th Cir. 1991). Because the child survived, manslaughter could not be charged. For the same reason, **answer D is not correct**. The best answer in this case is answer B. Many jurisdictions have created such classifications to punish actions exactly like the ones in this case, where the recklessness of the actor caused serious injury, but negligent homicide, manslaughter, and murder are unavailable as charges because the victim survived.

17.   **The correct answer is A.** The intent to injure here can be found under the doctrine of transferred intent. *People v. Scott*, 927 P.2d 288 (Cal. 1996). The most common explanation for this theory is that the necessary intent "follows" the action. If the defendant intended to punch someone, although he actually hit another person, he remains culpable in terms of the resulting injury. **Answer B is incorrect** because the statute explicitly requires proof of intent. No societal purpose would be served if answers C or D were true. If answer C were correct, the defendant would only be held responsible for his intentional acts if he had better skills at throwing punches. Similarly, if answer D were true, a defendant could be exonerated merely because the intended victim had been rude to the man who punched the actual victim. Thus, **answers C and D are incorrect.**

18.   **The correct answer is C.** In proving the mental state of knowledge, the key issue is whether the defendant herself knew the true nature of her activity. The issue is not whether a reasonable person would have known the activity was criminal (an objective standard) because knowledge requires a subjective determination. Therefore, **answer B is incorrect. Answer A is also incorrect,** as the government has conceded that Holly did not know of the criminal activities. **Answer D is wrong** because the statute requires a showing of knowledge, not intent.

19.   **The correct answer is C.** Most jurisdictions require that the defendant must have been personally aware of the risk involved in order to be convicted of criminal recklessness. *People v. Eckert*, 138 N.E.2d 794 (1956). This subjective requirement is much more stringent than the usual tort standard, which speaks of only a substantial deviation from the standard of care. Therefore, **answer B is not the best answer**. Answer A refers to the standard of negligence, which allows the finder of fact to conclude that a defendant should have been aware of the substantial, unjustifiable risk, and as a result finds him responsible. Recklessness, as noted above, means a personal, subjective awareness of the risk. Because this criminal statute does not adopt a negligence standard, **answer A is incorrect. Answer D is incorrect** for if Bill's behavior is found to be reckless in nature, he will likely be determined to have caused the child's injury.

20.   If Victoria did not mean to inflict harm upon her boyfriend, she will not likely be convicted of intentional wounding. The state of mind of intent requires that a defendant purposefully cause the harm prohibited by the crime. *State v. Smith*, 621

A.2d 493 (N.J. 1993). Regarding the facts of this case, Victoria does not appear to have acted with intent to harm. While the struggle might have been reckless due to the presence of the large knife, the requirement here involves far more than subjective awareness of a substantial risk. Unless the government can show a true purposeful act to harm the boyfriend, the prosecution will fail.

21. **Answer D is incorrect** in that the mistake presented here is one of fact, not one of law. Trisha believed she was entering her own apartment; she is not asserting that she believed breaking into her neighbor's apartment was legal. Often the distinctions between mistake of law and mistake of fact are less than clear, but not here. **Answer A is incorrect** in that mistake of fact does not provide an affirmative defense. An affirmative defense supposes that the accused is guilty of the crime, but for policy considerations—such as the conclusion that people should be able to provide a reasonable level of self-defense—the defendant can be exonerated. No such defense exists merely because the defendant was mistaken. **Answer C is also incorrect** because burglary requires an intent to enter someone else's dwelling. **Answer B provides the best response**. While Trisha cannot offer this evidence as a defense, she will likely be able to present evidence as to her mistake in order to negate the government's contention that she intended to break in and steal from her neighbor's apartment. Such an approach is an assertion that the government has failed to establish a required element of the crime, the element of intent. *United States v. Short*, 4 U.S.C.M.A. 437 (1954).

22. A showing of intent is required for the attempted murder charge, so the mere act of planting an explosive device that appeared dangerous on a train would not be enough to convict. The government must demonstrate beyond a reasonable doubt that it was the defendant's purpose to kill or seriously injure others. If the defendant is believed, he could avoid such a conviction, as he knew that the bomb could not explode. The argument that a killing would be impossible under the circumstances will provide no defense. The question relates to the defendant's knowledge, his intent. If he is believed as to his state of mind, he will prevail on this charge. If, however, he is not believed, the fact-finder could conclude that the defendant intentionally took all steps necessary to carry out his plan, and the defendant will be convicted of attempted murder.

23. **The best answer is C,** as courts typically do not allow the advice of private counsel to be used in defending against a criminal charge. Any other approach would put lawyers in an uncomfortable position because their clients could benefit from bad legal advice. *United States v. Tallmadge*, 829 F. 2d 767 (9th Cir. 1987). **Answer A is wrong**, for although his reliance appears reasonable, Jorge had the necessary *mens rea* to be found guilty of the crime. For that reason **answer B is also wrong**. Finally, because few crimes are strict liability, most probably the statute here would require at least knowledge of his actions. Thus, **answer D is also wrong**.

24. Yes. The result changes dramatically if Jorge has relied on a statement of the law given to him by an individual charged with construing or enforcing the law. Because a citizen could properly assume that the head of the Office on Environmental Control has the authority to give advice on a matter relating to pollution, Jorge's reliance

would be viewed as reasonable. It could, then, be offered as a defense of mistake of law. The courts consistently allow this defense under these circumstances, as to do otherwise would be to enable the government to prosecute citizens who properly and timely seek government approval of their actions. In a sense, the defense is truly an estoppel principle.

25. Under the common law, parties to a crime, those not as directly involved as the perpetrators of the crimes themselves, were criminally responsible based upon the premise that all culpable individuals should be punished. *Standefer v. United States*, 447 U.S. 10 (1980). For this reason, **answer A is not the correct response.** Under the common law, Tabitha can be held liable as a party to the crime, even though she was not directly involved in the criminal enterprise. A principal in the first degree must have committed at least one element of the crime in question and must have been present at the scene of the crime. Because keeping watch for the authorities is not an element of the crime of armed robbery, Tabitha would not be a principal in the first degree under common law rules, so **answer B is incorrect. The best answer is answer C** because Tabitha truly was a principal in the second degree. Under the common law, a principal in the second degree must have provided some assistance to the commission of the crime and must have been present at the scene of the crime. Although Tabitha could argue that she was not actually at the scene of the crime (that she was only having coffee next door), such an argument would likely prove unsuccessful as she was in the immediate vicinity. Thus, **answer D is not the best answer.** If, however, Tabitha were able to successfully argue that her presence at a café next door to the bank was not sufficient to make her present at the scene of the crime, answer D would be correct. Under the common law, a party would be considered an accessory before the fact if she provided some measure of assistance toward the commission of the crime, but was not at the scene of the crime. It is important to remember that the above-described common law distinctions have fallen out of favor, and relatively few jurisdictions maintain meaningful distinctions based on this rubric. Instead, the modern approach of a majority of jurisdictions in determining the liability of parties focuses on the defendant's state of mind and the level of assistance offered, as indicated below.

26. Under the modern approach regarding parties to crimes, a determination as to whether individuals other than the perpetrators are participants in crimes is judged by an involvement and intent standard. Tabitha's liability will be determined both by her activities and by her purpose to participate. *United States v. Batt*, 811 F. Supp. 625 (D. Kan. 1993). After considering these elements, a jury will be able to determine whether Tabitha can be held liable as an accessory after the fact, defined as a person who renders aid, comfort, and/or shelter to the criminal (even though she was not present at the commission of the crime). Although Tabitha's involvement in helping to hide the criminals would be sufficient to find her culpable as an accessory after the fact, her intent in relation to her actions must also be resolved. If Tabitha thought that her boyfriend was joking about robbing a bank, a jury could determine that she did not have the requisite intent, as judged by both objective and subjective standards, to participate in any part of the crime. If, however, Tabitha

knew that her boyfriend robbed banks in the past, and, for this reason, Tabitha truly understood that he was not joking about the reason he wanted to go to the cabin, Tabitha could be found to have the sufficient intent to be held responsible for assisting in the robbery after the fact.

27. **The best answer is answer C.** Under the modern approach, a person can be held liable as a party to a crime if the person's involvement in the crime and his intent to participate in the crime are shown. *State v. Gladstone*, 474 P.2d 274 (Wash. 1970). Stan was aware that Bill intended to harm Big Jim and he provided Bill with assistance in that endeavor by giving him Big Jim's address. Thus, Stan was sufficiently involved in the crime. In addition, from this information a jury could conclude that Stan intended for the crime to occur. **Answer B is not the best answer** because Stan's actions, together with his intent, are sufficient for him to be found liable as a party to the crime under the modern approach. Merely providing information to Bill without the intent that a crime occur would not be sufficient to establish liability for a party to a crime. However, in this case, Stan exhibited the requisite intent, given his knowledge and feelings. Because merely wishing injuries upon Big Jim would not warrant criminal liability, **answer D is not the most complete answer. Answer A is not the best answer** because a person need not commit an element of the crime to be held liable as a party to the crime. Virtually any action can be considered sufficient to establish guilt as a party to the crime if the person knew of the principal actor's intentions, as Stan did, and purposefully took actions in order to further those intentions, as Stan did.

28. No, Stan cannot be held liable for Bill's actions. While Stan's intent and actions may be clear, there is no causal link between them and the ultimate crime. While Stan might be guilty of other crimes—such as solicitation—he cannot be held as a party to the battery.

29. A person can be held liable as a party to the unplanned crime of another that occurs during the commission of a planned crime if that other crime could have been foreseen as a predictable occurrence associated with the planned crime. *People v. Poplar*, 173 N.W.2d 732 (Mich. App. 1969). **The correct answer is answer A.** Ellen did not intend for an assault to occur, only a burglary. Because the sexual assault of a woman in the house was not a natural and foreseeable consequence of the burglary Ellen intended, she will not be held responsible for the sexual assault, even though she may be held responsible as an accomplice to the burglary. Although Ellen committed an act in furtherance of the assault (driving Jason to the house), she did not know of or intend for the assault to occur, nor should she have foreseen the assault. For this reason, **answer B is incorrect. Answer D is also incorrect**. Ellen will not be held culpable as a party to the crime of assault because Jason did not act within the scope of the contemplated crime and because his actions were not foreseeable by Ellen (but not because she did not know that such actions would occur). **Answer C is an incomplete answer,** because it fails to examine which crime Ellen intended to commit together with her partner Jason.

30. Yes, Ellen can be considered responsible as an accomplice to the owner's murder. Unlike the sexual assault described above, the possibility of a violent altercation

with the homeowner in the process of burglarizing a home is a foreseeable consequence of the burglary. The fact finder can determine that Ellen has accepted the consequences of the burglary to the extent that they were foreseeable. On this basis, the jury could hold Ellen liable as an accomplice for the owner's murder because she could have reasonably anticipated such an event when her partner entered the house.

31. **The best answer is answer D.** Although Amanda could be seen to have encouraged Lance in his action, that view is only available in hindsight. Words alone will rarely demonstrate both the action and intent necessary to find one culpable as a party to a crime unless it can be shown that the person in question had some knowledge or belief that her words would encourage someone to commit a particular crime. Here, it is unlikely that Amanda meant for her comments to lead to violence. Although Lance was encouraged in his actions by the remarks Amanda made, that encouragement may not be enough to render Amanda guilty as a party to Lance's crime. Furthermore, there is no indication that Amanda intended for harm to come to Lance's boss, although she might have felt that the woman "deserved" it. Therefore, **answer A is incorrect**. Similarly, **answer B is not the best answer.** Because Amanda's remarks were not sufficient to create criminal liability in these circumstances, a clear showing of intent is also needed. *United States v. Garguilo*, 310 F.2d 249 (2nd Cir. 1969).

    Answer C is not the best answer, although it points to the possible constitutional argument against allowing a person's words to be held against her. However, the First Amendment's protection of speech is not absolute and this answer fails to address the nuances of such an argument. Under the Constitution, a person is entitled to criticize laws and to advocate the violation of criminal laws in an abstract sense. However, the First Amendment does not protect those who incite others to break the law by encouraging the commission of specific crimes. *United States v. Kelley*, 769 F.2d 215 (4th Cir. 1985). Although it is unlikely that Amanda could be found liable for her remarks, her lack of criminal liability results from the fact that her speech did not evince the requisite intent or incitement, not from any constitutional protections associated with her speech.

32. **The best answer is answer C.** Although many jurisdictions provide for the opportunity to abandon or withdraw from a criminal endeavor, Mike did not meet those requirements. In order to effectively withdraw, Mike would have had to voluntarily and completely relinquish his purpose and make a substantial effort to prevent the crime from taking place. *People v. Ozarowski*, 344 N.E.2d 370 (N.Y. 1976). This would have required Mike to tell the others of his intent to quit the project and to try to stop them in their purpose, probably by contacting the police. Because Mike did not take either of these actions, he did not withdraw from the kidnapping. As such, no matter the jurisdiction, Mike would likely incur liability as a party to the crime of kidnapping. For the same reason, **answer A is incorrect. Answer B is incorrect** because Mike did involve himself in the crime. In order to initially incur responsibility, the endeavor must have involved some preparation. Here, there was extensive preparation for the crime, in which Mike participated. **Answer D is also incorrect** because many jurisdictions provide an opportunity to withdraw.

33. Unlike Mike, who will clearly not be considered to have properly abandoned the enterprise, the issue of Aiden's abandonment is a bit more complicated. Aiden did attempt to end the endeavor by trying to dissuade Floyd from continuing in the plot. Aiden did contact the police, meeting the last requirement of abandonment. He would probably lose, nevertheless, for two reasons. First, the kidnapping was complete with the taking of the child, so that there was no pending crime from which to withdraw. Second, even if withdrawal was possible, whether his withdrawal from the enterprise was *voluntary* remains unclear. Generally, one is not considered to have *voluntarily* withdrawn from a crime unless one is motivated by a change of heart. *People v. Taylor*, 598 N.E.2d 693 (N.Y. 1992). This signifies, at least, that one should not by motivated by fear of failure in one's criminal goals or by a mere concern that arrest is imminent. To the extent that Aiden is able to convince a fact-finder that his altruistic goals were the motivating factors in his decision to abandon the plot, Aiden may be able to argue that he withdrew effectively.

34. No, Salma will lose the argument on appeal. Instinctively, her view makes sense. As one appeals judge put it, "there must be some dependency between aiding or abetting and the offense that is aided or abetted." The Supreme Court, however, took a very different view, allowing the conviction of the defendant to stand even though the other person was found not guilty of receiving the bribe. The Court concluded that so long as the jury in such a case found, beyond a reasonable doubt, both that the defendant gave a bribe and that it was received, it was appropriate to hold the defendant criminally responsible. The mere fact that another jury reached a different result in another prosecution is irrelevant. Such a situation "does no more than manifest the simple, if discomforting, reality that 'different juries may reach different results under any criminal statue. That is one of the consequences we accept under our jury system.' While symmetry of results may be intellectually satisfying, it is not required." *Standefer v. United States*, 447 U.S. 10 (1980).

[A]   Solicitation

35. To find Wendy guilty of solicitation, the government must prove that she intended the crime be committed and took some act in furtherance of the crime, usually in the form of active encouragement or inducement. *People v. Keen*, 214 S.E.2d 242 (N.C. 1975). While such intent is usually proven by circumstantial evidence, if the only evidence against her is a casual remark at a social gathering, Wendy is unlikely to be found guilty of solicitation. If, however, she was found to have intended that Peter murder his wife, and therefore found guilty of solicitation, her subsequent comment to Peter that she was not seriously suggesting he get rid of his wife will not defeat the solicitation charge. In most states, one cannot successfully withdrawal from a solicitation once sufficient encouragement has occurred. As soon as the suggestion or request has been made, the crime is complete, so a later change of heart will not bar her conviction of solicitation.

36. **The best answer is D.** The act requirement for solicitation is that a person request or encourage another to commit a crime. The crime also contains a mental state requirement, intent that the crime be committed. The difference between casual conversation and true solicitation to commit a crime is often one of degree, and therefore a conviction for solicitation may fail for a lack of intent even if a sufficient act might be shown. On these facts, it appears unlikely that the government could prove that Steven truly intended that Miguel commit this crime. However, with more concrete evidence of intent, Steven could indeed be found guilty of solicitation. Therefore, **answer B is incorrect**. For example, had Steven said to Mike, "You ought to give that guy what he deserves and slash his tires," the government might be able to prove he had the requisite state of mind. In such a case, answer B would be correct.

   Answer A is incorrect because it does not appear that Steven suggested that Miguel carry out the crime. **Answer C is incorrect** because solicitation does not require a significant or affirmative act toward the crime by the solicitor, only a statement or action manifesting encouragement or support for another committing that crime.

37. **The correct answer is A.** Regardless of whether or not the person solicited to commit the crime would accept the request or encouragement, if the elements are otherwise shown, the crime of solicitation has taken place. *People v. Gordon*, 120 Cal. Rptr. 840 (Cal. 1975). The reason for the criminalization of solicitation is to punish the culpable intent of the solicitor, so the ability or desire of another to act on the solicitation is irrelevant. Here, Samantha demonstrated the requisite intent to acquire drugs and requested that another person provide them, allowing her to be found guilty of solicitation. **Answer C is therefore incorrect. Answer B is**

wrong because the officer's status is irrelevant; the proof element goes to Samantha's state of mind. A payment of money could establish true intent for the solicitation, so **answer D is also incorrect**.

38. **The best answer is D.** Solicitation can take place without effectively communicating the request or encouragement to the intended person. As Tony believed he was soliciting the crime, he can be seen as just as culpable as if he had communicated the request to have Pete assaulted. Therefore, **answer C does not provide the best explanation**. It is possible Tony could argue he never intended to communicate the request because he knew the letter would not be mailed. **Answers A and B are wrong**, as they deny Tony's culpability in requesting Pete be injured, while both the intent and act requirements of solicitation appear to be met here.

39. **The best answer is C.** The woman's comment—after the other, earlier acts—that she was trying to make money, adds convincing circumstantial evidence that she intended to solicit prostitution, which is defined as performing sexual acts in exchange for a fee. While answer D might be correct, in that a jury or a judge perhaps could find the circumstantial evidence convincing enough to convict; the woman's comment makes the case much more clearly one of solicitation. Her comment establishes the intention behind her actions. Thus, **answer D is not the best answer**.

    Answer A is incorrect because circumstantial evidence can establish guilt for any crime. *People v. Scott*, 1 Cal. Rptr. 600 (Cal. App. 1960). Usually, the difficulty in obtaining convictions lies in establishing intent through circumstantial evidence, but in this case, the woman's statement to the officers effectively resolves any doubt concerning her state of mind (i.e., she was not just being friendly or looking for a date if she was hoping to make money from her actions.). Therefore, **answer B is also incorrect**.

[B] Attempt

40. **The best answer is B.** The attempt offense requires both the intent to commit the crime and a substantial act in furtherance of the crime. Although his intent to murder his father may be clear from his writings and his considered plan, George had not yet tried to implement his plan. Action toward the crime is required for attempt because the law does not penalize bad thoughts alone. **Answer D is not correct** because it improperly considers the writing of the journal itself to be the act in furtherance of the crime. Such an expression is insufficient. While jurisdictions vary as to the act requirement, almost all would require either a substantial step toward the commission of the murder (Model Penal Code and majority view) or an act in relatively close proximity to the completed crime. *People v. Mahboubian*, 543 N.E.2d 34 (N.Y. 1989). The mere recording of George's thoughts in a journal would appear too minor an act to qualify for an attempt conviction in most states. **Answer A is wrong** because—from the journal—George's intent was clear. The problem here related to the act, not the mental state. **Answer C is not correct** because George took no action to implement the plan.

41.   **The best answer is B.** The crime of attempt requires intent. The mother may have acted recklessly, or with knowledge of the ramifications of her actions, allowing for a conviction for the crime of involuntary manslaughter had the child died. The child, however, did not die. Involuntary manslaughter is defined as an unintentional killing. Attempt, however, requires a higher state of mind. The mother's mental state would not allow for a finding of attempt for she did not intend the killing. Therefore, one cannot be convicted of attempted involuntary manslaughter. *Bailey v. Nevada*, 688 P.2d 320 (1984). As such, **answers C and D are incorrect. Answer A is wrong** because it fails to recognize that multiple parties can be held responsible for a single crime.

42.   No. The crime of attempt seeks to punish culpable individuals who have moved in the direction of committing a crime, coupled with a serious purpose to achieve that end. Lying in wait and getting ready to commit a crime would be viewed in most jurisdictions as evidence of a substantial step toward the commission of a crime, or an act in close proximity to the commission of a crime. *People v. Staples*, 85 Cal. Rptr. 589 (Cal. App. 1970). It would, thus, satisfy the act requirement for the crime of attempt. Still, the government must also demonstrate that Ros intended to commit the crime. If she were to say nothing, and there were no prior incidents between the parties, the mere fact that she was at the house with a weapon would not show, beyond a reasonable doubt, the high state of mind needed for a successful attempt prosecution. Such a state of mind could be shown with prior altercations between Ros and her boss, threats made by Ros, statements made by her to others about her intent to harm her boss, and so on. On these facts, however, conviction is unlikely.

43.   From Doug's actions, it seems the *mens rea* requirement of intent could be met in his case. The major question in Doug's prosecution will be whether he committed a sufficient act toward the completion of the crime. Very few states allow *any* act in furtherance to meet the act requirement for attempt. To do so might permit possibly innocent persons, and those with only vague or momentary criminal intentions, to be convicted of a crime without these people having genuinely committed themselves to the criminal enterprise. Most jurisdictions require that some significant act toward the commission of the intended crime be taken in order for one to be guilty of an attempted crime. This requirement ensures that culpable actions are punished, rather than bad thoughts alone. If the apartment were truly rented out for the purpose of facilitating the crime or the escape from the crime, Doug may have taken the necessary substantial step, particularly when it is coupled with the hiring of a safecracking expert. In addition, Doug was deterred from carrying out his plan only due to the actions of law enforcement and this will not aid in his resisting the attempt charge. *United States v. Shelton*, 30 F.3d 702 (6th Cir. 1994).

44.   **The best answer is A.** The situation presented in this example could be best characterized as a case of factual impossibility. This argument has never been permitted as a defense. *People v. Dlugash*, 363 N.E.2d 1155 (N.Y. 1977). There would be no justification to allow this person to escape culpability because fortuity prevented the ultimate crime. Julia displayed her dangerousness to society very clearly. Her act demonstrated this unequivocally, and had she been successful, she

would in fact have violated the law. **Answer B is not the best answer** because it does not truly deal with the impossibility issue. **Answer C is also incorrect** because it entirely ignores the issue. Julia took every act possible to ensure the killing would occur had it not been prevented by her own stupidity or mistake. Under the doctrine of factual impossibility, a defendant can be found guilty regardless of whether ultimate success was a real possibility. Thus, **answer D is not correct**.

45. **B is the correct answer** if Julia genuinely thought she could commit the murder and took a substantial step toward that crime. Factual impossibility, as noted above, is no defense to the attempt charge. Therefore, **answer C is clearly wrong**. **Answer A is also wrong**, as most states do not allow *any* action to be the basis for the crime of attempt. Instead, the action must be substantial or major. **Answer D is incorrect**, as the elements of the attempt crime can be satisfied even if the elements of burglary can also be shown. There is no bar to charging the defendant with both crimes.

46. **Answer B is the best answer.** Rebecca's actions fulfill the requirements of attempt. **Answer A is wrong** because it incorrectly represents the purpose and scope of criminal law, for we do not punish individuals for bad thoughts alone. Individuals who act upon those bad thoughts, however, are prosecuted. Here, Rebecca may be convicted of attempted murder, because she not only wished her aunt to die, but took affirmative steps to fulfill that wish. Rebecca's decision to abandon her plan, after administering the pills, would not provide a defense to attempted murder. Thus, **answer C is incorrect**. Significantly, Rebecca did not abandon her plan before the final step of giving her aunt the pills. Rather, it was only after she discovered her mistake, after the crime of attempt was already completed (when she would have successfully killed her aunt had there been no mistake on her part), that Rebecca changed her mind. No withdrawal is possible *after* the final criminal act has taken place. **Answer D is incorrect**, for it invokes again the concept of factual impossibility. Because her aunt would have died had Rebecca been correct as to the contents of the pills, it was a mere fortuity, which prevented the killing. As such, it falls within the doctrine of factual impossibility, and that is no defense to an attempt charge.

[C]   Conspiracy

47. **The correct answer is A.** In a majority of states and in the federal system, a conspiracy to commit an offense does not merge with the substantive crime. *Pinkerton v. United States*, 328 U.S. 640 (1946). This means that Sybil and John can be convicted of both kidnapping and conspiracy to commit the kidnapping. The merger rule for conspiracy differs from attempt and solicitation, which generally do merge with the completed offenses. Thus **answer C is wrong**. This difference for conspiracy is based on the view that groups are more dangerous than individuals in terms of planning crimes. Moreover, merger is not mandated, as the very separate element of agreement needed for conspiracy is not present for the completed offense.

Answer B accurately reflects the rule in a minority of states, which dictates that the charges for conspiracy and the substantive crime be merged. Most states, though, do not follow this principle. Thus, **answer B is not the best answer. Answer D is wrong** because it incorrectly invokes the double jeopardy protections of the 5th and 14th Amendments. Punishment for the conspiracy charge and a charge of a substantive crime does not violate the Constitution in that each of the charges involves a distinct crime with separate elements. Conspiracy requires an agreement while the substantive offense requires the completed act of kidnapping. *Pinkerton v. United States*, 328 U.S. 640 (1946).

48. **The correct answer is B.** Although no express agreement could be shown here, none is required for a conspiracy. The requisite agreement can be inferred from the circumstances. In fact, explicit agreements are rarely found. Usually conspiracy convictions have foundations in implied agreements, proven only with convincing circumstantial evidence. *People v. Mariano*, 934 P.2d 315 (N.M. 1997). Therefore, **answers A and C are incorrect**. Here, Lauren's complicity in Erika's actions could be inferred from the eye contact, by her inaction in the store, and by their running from the store together. A jury may find that her laughter signaled support for Erika's actions, and that in looking around, she was actually serving as a look out. For these reasons, **answer D is also incorrect** because these circumstances could warrant a finding that Lauren acted out of an implicit understanding to rob the store.

49. **Answer A is the correct response.** The modern trend, based on the Model Penal Code, only requires that the person accused of conspiracy agree with another person. The government, under this view, need not show that any other person was in agreement. Therefore, Thomas can be convicted of conspiracy if he believed that he was acting pursuant to an understanding with Kate, even if Kate did not truly share his criminal intent. Under this so-called unilateral approach, it is no defense if the other party to the supposed agreement never intended to agree, is acquitted, or is immune from prosecution. Even though there was no genuine agreement here, the unilateral approach allows society to hold Thomas culpable for his actions and for his intent, under the circumstances as he believed them to be. *State v. St. Christopher*, 232 N.W.2d 798 (Minn. 1975). Because an actual agreement is not required under the modern approach, **answer B is incorrect**.

    Answer C accurately reflects the common law approach to the agreement element, but not the Model Penal Code, modern trend in conspiracy law. Thus **Answer C is not the best answer**. Under this bilateral view, at least two people must agree to commit a criminal act to be found guilty of conspiracy. That is, at least two people must share a criminal intent. Without such a shared agreement, Thomas could be guilty of solicitation, but not conspiracy. **Answer D is incorrect** in that it presents a possible defense of factual impossibility. As with attempt and solicitation, factual impossibility provides no defense to a conspiracy charge.

50. **The correct answer is B.** The general rule is that a true agreement must be shown as the basis for a conspiracy conviction. Beth's sale of the drugs to Joel does not fulfill the chief requirement for conspiracy, as there was no true agreement. Thus, **answer A is incorrect**, unless the case was brought in a jurisdiction following the "unilateral approach," as indicated above. Generally, the crime of conspiracy does not merge with the completed offense, so that should present no bar to conviction.

For this reason, **answer C is incorrect**. Answer **D is also not the right answer**, because the defense of entrapment generally requires more of a government inducement than is present here, as discussed below.

51.   Although it is possible that Zeb could be convicted of conspiracy on the indicated facts, it is unlikely without further evidence of his knowledge and intent. It may be difficult to prove that Zeb knew why Betty wanted the plastic bags. If there was further proof that Zeb was involved in the drug operation on a regular basis, a prosecutor may be able to demonstrate his intent in that Zeb provided Betty the necessary information to make the sale that day. Without such proof that the boyfriend at least had knowledge of the transaction taking place, no agreement can be inferred from the circumstances. If Zeb had been in the room when Betty made the deal with Joel, for example, an agreement could be implied from the circumstances. In such a case, the requisite evidence would be in place to find the couple engaged in a conspiracy or a joint operation to sell drugs. While the government's case seems strong against Betty for sale of the drugs, without additional evidence, Zeb should escape a conviction for conspiracy.

The key here is that the government must prove that Zeb was aware that Betty was selling drugs. An agreement could then be inferred from the circumstances, but only because Zeb had knowledge of Betty's illegal activity. If knowledge could be shown, intent might be inferred from his offering of assistance. A jury could then conclude that Betty and Zeb had at least tacitly agreed to sell the drugs.

52.   **The best answer is D.** While Karry's action in this transaction may lend itself to aiding and abetting more than a conspiracy charge, an agreement could be inferred from Karry's repeated sales to Reggie with the teenagers present. Unlike a one-time purchase, which may not allow such an inference to be drawn, under these circumstances, a fact-finder might conclude that Karry knew Reggie's intent. As she knew that he was to use the alcohol illegally, her tacit agreement to sell to him repeatedly could demonstrate her intent to make the sale. *Direct Sales Co. v. United States*, 319 U.S. 703 (1943). Therefore, **answer A is incorrect**. Moreover, **answer C is not the best answer** because intent can be found from circumstantial evidence. The facts here suggest that Karry might have wished to sell her merchandise to the teens, as long as the sale itself could be viewed as legitimate. Unless Karry can demonstrate she had no knowledge of Reggie's actions or intentions, it appears a jury could find she intended the crime Reggie committed. **Answer B is not entirely true**, for if Karry did possess the knowledge that the crime be carried out, or intended that underage individuals could purchase alcohol from her through some means, she can be held criminally responsible.

53.   **The best answer is D.** Conspiracy requires both the intent to agree to carry out a crime and the intent that the crime be committed. In general, criminal agents are responsible for the foreseeable ramifications of their actions. *Pinkerton v. United States*, 328 U.S. 640 (1946). In this case, while it appears that the group had purposefully agreed to attack Marco, the prosecution would have to prove that the group intended to kill Marco for the charge of conspiracy to commit murder to be valid. The individual members of the group may have some criminal liability for

murder or manslaughter, in that their actions may be found to be so reckless that they can be held responsible for Marco's death. But conspiracy to commit murder is a distinct offense requiring the intents to agree and to kill. Because such intents could not be proven here, **answer B is wrong**.

Answer C is incorrect because the government likely could show that the group agreed to beat up Marco. As discussed above, an agreement can be inferred from the circumstances. **Answer A is incorrect** because the intent relates to an attack, not necessarily to a homicide. If the government was able to establish that the intent of the group was to kill Marco, then a conviction of conspiracy to commit murder would be possible. Yet, it is more likely that this group did not intend Marco's death and only acted with a reckless disregard of the impact of their actions. As these answers show, the state of mind requirement for conspiracy can be higher than for the substantive criminal object of the conspiracy, precluding a conviction of conspiracy in some situations although the crime itself may have been committed while acting in concert with others.

54. **The correct answer is B.** As long as Steve acted in furtherance of the conspiracy, and as long as those actions were foreseeable, the liability for those actions are attributed to Catherine unless she affirmatively withdrew, see below. The justification for this expansive liability rests on the foundation that conspiracy is intended to punish criminals acting in concert. In criminal law, people are held responsible for the full consequences of their actions, as long as those consequences can be seen as foreseeable results of the criminal activity. *Pinkerton v. United States*, 328 U.S. 640 (1946). In this situation, Steve's financial trouble and resulting expanded operations in the drug trade were clearly foreseeable. Thus, **answer C is incorrect**. The network in place at the time of Steve's arrest seems a likely result of an addict managing a small-scale drug operation. **Answer A is incorrect** because Catherine's liability is limited to foreseeable, not all, consequences. Catherine's distance from the operation will not absolve her of liability, so **answer D is incorrect**.

55. **The best answer is A.** Although Catherine's actions may not satisfy the requirements of abandonment for the crime of conspiracy, in most states, such withdrawal limits liability for later crimes. Therefore, **answers C and D are incorrect. Answer B is also incorrect**, as withdrawal is generally effective only if affirmative actions are taken in addition to notice. *United States v. Riebold*, 135 F.3d 1226 (8th Cir. 1998).

56. **The correct answer is B.** A conspirator will be held responsible for the conspiracy as long as any of its members perpetuate the conspiracy through the commission of an overt act. Any act, however minor, taken by any conspirator will keep the statute of limitations from running. *United States v. O'Brien*, 131 F.3d 1428 (10th Cir. 1997). This demonstrates another way in which conspiracy law can have a wider scope in punishing culpable individuals than other areas of criminal law. **Answer A is an incorrect statement** of the operation of statutes of limitations. They provide a bar to prosecution if the required amount of time has elapsed. **Answer C is also wrong.** While it correctly states the law, it is inapplicable to this case, as actions were taken during the period. As explained above, **answer D is wrong**. The scope

of conspiracy liability extends beyond one individual in order to make all actors responsible for the foreseeable acts of others, even with regard to the use of the statute of limitations.

57. Jackson may very well be convicted of murder if the killing is viewed as foreseeable under either an aiding and abetting theory or a conspiracy claim. Conviction for conspiracy to commit murder, however, seems highly unlikely. The joint action in the beating of Sheldon could give rise to an inference of agreement to injure the victim. Jackson's intent to do harm to Sheldon is clear, but an intent to kill the victim by knifing him is not so apparent on Jackson's part. Jackson could be held substantially responsible for the foreseeable criminal actions of his co-conspirator Cooper, which might include the killing. Neither Cooper nor Jackson can likely be convicted of conspiracy to commit murder, however, for the prosecution must prove that each party intended to carry out an agreement to kill the victim at that time and the facts do not seem to support such a showing.

58. **Answer D is the correct answer**, for if the prosecution is brought under one general conspiracy statute, the one agreement can only be the basis for one charge. *Braverman v. United States*, 317 U.S. 49 (1942). Therefore, both **answers A and B are incorrect**. Even in those statutes that require overt acts (and federal drug conspiracy statutes generally do not), any act, however minimal, will suffice, making **answer C incorrect**.

59. **Answer B is the correct answer**, as the Supreme Court has held that the key is the legislative intent that is demonstrated with the presence of distinct conspiracy statutes dealing with related activities. *Albernaz v. United States*, 450 U.S. 333 (1981). In this case, the Court held, such a prosecution would not violate Double Jeopardy principles, thus making **answer D incorrect**. The prosecution would be valid, even though a single agreement would form the basis for showing violations of three distinct statutes. **Answer A, therefore, would be incorrect, as would answer C.**

[A] The Property Offenses: Larceny, Embezzlement, False Pretenses

60. **The best answer is A.** John met all of the requirements of larceny, including intent to steal. This intent could be demonstrated by all of his actions. The taking element is satisfied by the slightest movement away from the premises. *Smith v. United States*, 291 F.2d 220 (9th Cir. 1961). **Answer B is wrong** because while there was not a successful actual theft of the coat, the taking element has been shown. Removing the goods—at all—from the owner's control satisfies the offense requirement. As such, **answer D is incorrect**. **Answer C is also incorrect** because although John had the store's consent in entering the store, that consent did not extend to theft. The trespass requirement does not allow those who have falsely gained consent of the owner to enter to escape liability.

61. **The best answer is A.** Juanita was in "possession" of the plant, meaning that she had authority regarding the legitimate use and maintenance of the good, a key requirement for embezzlement. *State v. Frasher*, 265 S.E.2d 43 (W. Va. 1980). **Answer B is wrong**, as larceny involves a theft committed by someone not in possession, but only in mere custody, of the good. **Answer C is also wrong,** as title did not pass here (the rightful owner was not giving the plant to Juanita). Although Juanita was the manager, she was not authorized to sell goods for her personal use. **Answer D is not correct**, a robbery is defined as the taking of property by force or threat of force, not present here.

62. Amy's actions, while not larceny in the most common sense, satisfy all of the required elements of that crime. The first element, trespass, is met because although Amy was invited onto the premises by the restaurant, it was on the condition that she would pay for her meal. Her conduct constitutes trespass. *People v. Manning*, 197 N.W.2d 152 (Mich. App. 1972). In eating her meal, she accomplished a taking and the asportation element could be considered met as she left the restaurant full of free food. The food was the personal property of the restaurant, as it only provided the meal on the condition that she would pay. Whether Amy had the intent to steal would be the most problematic element to prove. Increasingly, the law looks to the intent of the defendant at the time of the flight to determine whether there was a larceny committed. The common law focused on the intent to steal at the time of the initial taking, here the eating. Amy, of course, did not have that intention at the start. However, the proper solution in such a situation is not to merely leave without payment, but to return to pay for the meal or to make other such arrangements. Once she decided to leave the restaurant without paying, Amy did form the intent to steal. Today, most courts would conclude that this action constitutes larceny.

63. **The correct answer is A.** The elements for embezzlement differ slightly from jurisdiction to jurisdiction, but returning the money will never be sufficient to absolve the defendant from liability. Once the money is taken and put to one's own use, the offense is complete. Another consistent element of embezzlement is that the defendant was in a fiduciary or trust relationship with the property taken. *State v. Brown*, 422 S.E.2d 489 (W. Va. 1992). As Thomas was able to appropriate the money for his own use by virtue of his employment relationship with the bank, his actions meet the criteria of embezzlement. Generally, the elements of embezzlement require such an employee relationship and the taking or fraudulent conversion—for however short a period—of the property of another, with the intent to deprive the owner of its use. Here, Thomas' actions met all of these requirements and, therefore, he will likely be found guilty of embezzlement. Therefore, **answers B and D are incorrect**. In taking the money, Thomas was involved in the employment relationship even if he acted beyond the scope of his authority. Thus, **answer C is wrong**.

64. Intent forms one of the elements of embezzlement, but the intent to take or fraudulently convert property to one's own use—the state of mind needed for embezzlement—could be established by the circumstances. A jury could find that Daniel knew he was not authorized to give these special favors to his friends rather than his clients. By giving favors to his friends, he intended to take profits and property from his employer. As such, **answer A is incorrect. Answer B is similarly flawed** in that embezzlement often covers not only money but property as well. *State v. Childs*, 576 A.2d 42 (N.J. Super. AD 1990). While the phones were property, the discounted service resulted in less money going to the company, and could be considered money in any event. For these reasons, **answer C is the best answer**. The statute in the jurisdiction will determine whether such action is considered embezzlement, but property is almost always included as well as money in embezzlement actions. **Answer D is incorrect** in that it suggests that the company decides whether a particular action is embezzlement. While the company will have some role in the prosecution, once the employee misconduct is brought to the attention of the authorities, it is the government, which must decide whether to bring criminal charges.

65. **The best answer is C.** The crime of false pretenses requires that the defendant *knowingly* misrepresent a past or present material fact with the *intent* to defraud. *People v. Whight*, 43 Cal. Rptr. 2d 163 (Cal. App. 1995). While Gary certainly would fit these requirements, Stephanie was unaware of the fraud. Therefore, Stephanie lacked the *mens rea* for false pretenses. Stephanie did misrepresent material facts and was engaged in deceiving investors, but she was unaware of the falsity of her statements. While she may have been stupid, Stephanie did not intend fraudulent action. **Answers A and B are incorrect** for this reason. **Answer D is also incorrect**, as the misrepresentation was of a past or present fact. Although the main misrepresentation here would clearly be the ultimate plan to construct a retirement community, the investors were convinced to participate based on the statements that the land had been purchased and roads had been constructed. Of course, while Stephanie will likely not be convicted due to her lack of the required state of mind, Gary could be found criminally responsible.

[B]   Offenses Against the Habitation: Burglary, Arson

66.   **The best answer is A.** Under the common law definition of burglary, six elements must be met: (1) breaking, (2) entering, (3) at night, (4) in the dwelling house, (5) of another, (6) with intent to commit a felony inside. *State v. Bray*, 365 S.E.2d 571 (N.C. 1988). **Answer D is not correct**, as the law does not distinguish between early and late night break-ins. Burglary involves more than a mere robbery in the home, so **answer B is not the best answer**. The breaking requirement demands the creation of some opening to gain entry, and in this case the perpetrator gained access with the homeowner's assistance. Courts have long recognized entry by threat to be a breaking, hence all the elements of the crime have been met making A the correct answer. **Answer C, then, is not right**.

67.   **Answer B is correct,** as the common law required a break-in at night. Thus, **answer A is incorrect**. Most modern statutes do not have a nighttime break-in element. *People v. Hill*, 429 P.2d 586 (Cal. 1967). Thus, **answer C could be correct,** depending on your jurisdiction.

68.   The key requirements for arson include the malicious burning of the dwelling of another. While other persons' dwellings were burned here, it is unlikely that the malice requirement can be satisfied. Curtis was certainly negligent in tossing the lit cigarette. Malice, however, normally involves an intentional or clearly foreseeable burning. *People v. Lee*, 33 Cal. Rptr. 2d 782 (Cal. App. 1994). Curtis was foolish and unreasonable; he was not, however, malicious. He is, therefore, not guilty of arson.

69.   **Answer D is the correct answer**, as arson requires some burning, some flame of fire however slight, except in some modern statutes, which have expanded the common law definition. *Jones v. United States*, 529 U.S. 848 (2000). Thus, **Answer A is incorrect**. **Answer B is wrong**, as no entry is needed for an arson. **Answer C is also incorrect** because the entire structure does not have to be destroyed. Fire is the key to arson. Without it here, the crime may well be attempted arson.

[C]   Homicide

[1]   Killing

70.   **The best answer is B.** Under the common law, a death must occur within one year and a day of the underlying event for the perpetrator to be found guilty of murder. The "year and a day" rule originally existed because of problems in showing causation between an act and a death when a long period of time had elapsed. This rule creates an artificial limit on the ability to prove causation and assumes that a causal connection cannot be proven if the death occurs over one year and one day after the act. In many jurisdictions, the "year and a day" common law rule is still valid. Because Keesha died about thirteen months after Sam fired the shot, he cannot be convicted of murder under the common law. Given the ability of modern technology to prolong life, some states have eliminated the common law rule. In those states, the causal relationship between an act and a death must still be proven,

which often will become more difficult as time passes. Nonetheless, the mere number of days that elapsed between the date Keesha was shot and the day she died would not preclude Sam from being convicted of murder in states that have rejected the common law rule. Although Sam intended to kill Keesha and she died as a direct result of his actions, **answer A is not correct**. Under the common law "year and a day" rule, a death must occur within 366 days of the act.

Murder does not necessarily require the intent to kill. Murder is the unlawful killing of another person with malice. Malice is established by: (1) the intent to kill; (2) the intent to inflict great bodily harm; (3) gross recklessness (implied malice); or (4) the waiver of malice because the death occurred during the commission of a felony (felony murder). Sam intended to inflict great bodily harm. On this basis, Sam could be found to have malice sufficient for him to be found guilty of murder. *State v. Thompson*, 578 So.2d 1151 (La. App. 1991). However, as with answer A, **answer C is incorrect** because the "year and a day" rule cuts off liability even where the requisite mental state and causation exist. **Answer D is not correct**. Criminal law operates under the assumption that sane people can commit heinous acts. The mere fact that Sam shot Keesha is insufficient to establish an insanity defense.

71. **Answer A is the best answer.** Murder is the unlawful killing of a person with malice. Killing is causing another person's death. It is impossible to kill a person who is already dead. Because John was already dead when Jane shot him, she did not cause his death and could not be found guilty of John's murder. *People v. Dlugash*, 363 N.E.2d 1155 (N.Y. 1977).

Whether Jane's actions may or may not have been sufficient to kill John if he had been alive is irrelevant. Because John was already dead, Jane could not have killed him under any circumstances. The unlawful killing of another person with malice is one of the basic elements of the crime of murder. For this reason, **answers B and C are not correct**. **Answer D is not the best answer** because the elements of the crime of murder have not been established. Although, Jane had the intent to kill, she did not commit the act necessary for murder. Bad thoughts alone are not criminalized. Although she cannot be convicted of murder, she has probably violated other laws, perhaps even attempted murder. See, e.g., *Dlugash*, 363 N.E.2d at 1158-59.

72. **Answer D is the best answer.** According to the common law, a baby must be born alive to be considered a person under the law of homicide. *Keeler v. Superior Court*, 470 P.2d 617 (Cal. 1970). Because the crime of murder involves the killing of a person, Jack cannot be convicted of the baby's death if it was not born alive. This rule, which evolved during a period when it was difficult to discern the cause of a fetus's death, stated that a person could not be found guilty of murdering a fetus. Although Jack's intentions and actions would have been sufficient for him to be convicted of murder if the baby was born alive, those same actions and intentions would not be sufficient to convict Jack of murder if the baby was born dead.

Although Jack had the intent to kill, he did not commit the act of killing under the common law. The crime of murder requires a killing of a person, which could not occur under the common law if the baby was never alive. Because life does not begin until birth under the common law, Jack killed a fetus—not a person. Therefore, **answer A is incorrect. Answer B is not correct** because the timing of the act in relation to the birth is irrelevant. In the scenario in which the baby is born alive and then dies a short time after, the important inquiry is whether a causal connection can be made between the act and the death, even if that act occurred before the baby's birth. **Answer C is not correct** because it does not distinguish between the two fact patterns. A causal connection must always be established between an act and a death to establish the crime of murder. The common law rule assumes that the death of a fetus was not the result of the act. For this reason, if a baby is born dead, any act that occurred prior to the child's birth cannot be an element of the crime of murder. If, however, the baby is born alive and dies later, Jack may be convicted of murder if the act caused the baby's death.

73. Yes. Feticide statutes make the killing of a fetus illegal. In states that have enacted such laws, it would be possible for Jack to be convicted of the murder of a fetus based on harm caused to the fetus *in utero* regardless of whether the baby is born alive or stillborn.

74. **Answer C is the best answer.** At common law, death was defined as the cessation of respiratory and cardiac function. Thus, under the common law, James would not have been considered dead when the doctors removed his life support. Under many modern statutes, however, death is defined as the loss of all reflexes or brain activity. *State v. Fierro*, 603 P.2d 74 (Az. 1979). Because James was legally dead at the time his life support was removed, the doctors could not be considered an intervening cause of his death. Under modern statutes, James's death would be the result of the act that caused the trauma, which was the car accident.

Although answer A would be the best answer under the common law, death has been statutorily redefined in the modern statutes as noted above. Thus, **answer A is not the best answer**. While it may be tempting to say that the doctors hastened James's death, modern statutes define death as brain death. Because James was legally dead when the doctors disconnected the life support, **answer B is not correct. Answer D is not the best answer**. If a car accident is caused by truly reckless behavior it may well be the basis of an involuntary manslaughter, or even murder, as discussed below.

[2] Murder

75. **Answer A is the best answer.** An act that causes death must be committed with malice in order for a person to be convicted of murder. As noted above, malice is defined as: (1) the intent to kill; (2) the intent to commit serious bodily injury; (3) gross recklessness (implied malice); or (4) a crime committed during the commission of a felony. The malice element of murder can be established by an act that creates a very high probability of death or serious bodily injury. *Brinkley v. State*, 233 A.2d 56 (Del. 1967). Driving at extremely high speeds creates a very high probability of death. On this basis, Amy could be found guilty of murder. Driving over the speed limit but at lower speeds may be unreasonably risky, which could result in a charge of involuntary manslaughter.

Answer B is not correct because prior intent that has been abandoned is not relevant to an act that occurs later. Although malice can be implied from Amy's reckless behavior, it cannot be satisfied from an abandoned intent to kill. Bess did not have control over the car after Amy began speeding. When Bess got into the car, she did not know that Amy was going to drive at dangerously high speeds. She did not voluntarily expose herself to the extreme danger and was not free to get out of the car once the car was speeding down the road. Thus, **answer C is wrong. Answer D is not correct** because Amy knew that driving that fast was extremely dangerous; in fact, she was driving fast because she found the danger exhilarating. As Amy knew that her behavior was extremely risky, malice can be shown by gross recklessness.

76. **Answer C is the best answer.** At common law, an omission to act is normally not criminal. Under most circumstances, the criminal law does not require strangers to act in the behalf of others. A failure to act is only criminal under the common law when a legal duty to act exists. Such a legal duty to act can be created by statute or by contract. *Commonwealth v. Pestinikas*, 617 A.2d 1339 (Sup. Ct. Pa. 1992). Because Michael entered into an employment contract to take care of Jolinda, he can be held criminally liable for his failure to care for her. Hence, **answer A is incorrect**.

    A failure to act can be the cause of death as much as an affirmative act. Where there is a duty, the failure to act fulfills the *actus reus* element of the crime, and no overt act is required. **Answer B is incorrect** because Michael's failure to act, in violation of his legal duty to act, was the cause of Jolinda's malnutrition that resulted in her death. An omission to act is not criminal where only a moral duty to act, and not a legal duty, exists. Societal norms do not define the elements of a crime. **Answer D is incorrect** because Michael's failure to act on a moral duty does not make him a criminal. Here, Michael can be found criminally liable only because of his legal duty to act, not because he had a moral obligation to care for Jolinda.

77. Murder is an illegal killing with malice. The clearest way to demonstrate malice is the intent to kill. Here, Leonard acted out of his intent to kill the woman upstairs. He knew that telling the woman that her daughter was dead would be a terrible shock and would probably kill her due to her heart condition. Although the heart attack was the precise cause of her death, Leonard's words are the legal cause of her death. By uttering those words, he instigated the heart attack. Even an act as small as saying a few words can be the cause of death, so long as malice can be established. Leonard's planning demonstrates premeditation and deliberation. On this basis, he can be found guilty of first degree murder, as explained below.

78. **The best answer is answer B.** For the crime of murder, the government must show an intent to kill; an intent to commit serious bodily injury; gross recklessness; or that a killing occurred during the commission of a felony. Under this definition, it is unlikely that a jury could find that Abdul committed murder. Because it would be possible for Abdul to be convicted of murder, even if he did not intend to kill Eric, **answer A is not the best answer**. As explained above, if a jury found that Abdul had the intent to commit serious bodily injury, he could be convicted of murder.

Answer C is incorrect because, based on the facts, it does not appear that Abdul intended to commit serious bodily injury to Eric. Instead, Abdul was just caught up in the excitement. He did not intend to seriously injure anyone, just give a few black eyes. A finding of malice based upon the intent to commit serious bodily injury must be more that an intent to inflict some injury. An intent to simply injure that unexpectedly results in death would result in a conviction for involuntary manslaughter, not murder. The gross recklessness element is also called a "depraved heart" or "malignant heart" murder. Gross recklessness is behavior so dangerous that it demonstrates a disregard for life; however, it does not have to be behavior that is almost certain to cause death. Merely reckless behavior is insufficient to establish the malice element required for murder. Because answer D misstates the recklessness requirement for murder, **answer D is not the correct answer.**

79. The result might well change with these new facts. Normally people engaged in a fight which results in death are acting with some recklessness or negligence resulting in a charge of—at most—either involuntary manslaughter or negligent homicide. When, however, the defendant is so large and is so well trained in fighting, he may be charged with knowledge of the extreme risk his fighting entails. A trier of fact could, then, find that his participation in a brawl constitutes gross recklessness allowing for a conclusion that he killed the victim with implied malice. He could be convicted, on this basis, of murder. *People v. Bias*, 195 S.E.2d 626 (W. Va. 1973).

80. **Answer B is the best answer.** Murder is the unlawful killing of another person with malice. Intent to kill, intent to commit great bodily harm, gross recklessness (implied malice), and felony murder are the four ways to establish the malice mental state for murder. The man did not intend to kill or to commit great bodily harm, and he was not being reckless. The only remaining way to establish murder would be felony murder. Felony murder is an unlawful killing that occurs during the commission of a violent felony. *People v. Hackman*, 319 N.E.2d 511 (Ill. 1974). Because larceny of a book bag is not a violent felony, the man cannot be found guilty of felony murder.

Although the man did not intend to hit and kill the pedestrian, intent to kill is only one of four ways to establish the requisite mental state for murder. Because answer A only addresses this one possibility, **answer A is not the best answer**. In most jurisdictions, a crime is not complete until the criminal has reached a place of safety. In these circumstances, most jurisdictions would consider the library's parking lot to be part of the crime scene. The man would not be considered to be in a place of safety. If the man had committed a violent felony in the library, hitting a pedestrian in the parking lot might have been a killing during the commission of a violent felony, which would be a felony murder. Larceny of a book bag is not a violent felony, however, so **answer C is not correct**. Hitting a pedestrian when driving at a slow speed does not constitute gross recklessness. **Answer D is incorrect** because accidents can and do happen. Not all incidents involving an automobile hitting a pedestrian are necessarily the result of gross recklessness.

81. **Answer C is the best answer**. A killing committed during the commission of a violent felony is felony murder. The definition of a violent, or inherently dangerous

felony varies by jurisdiction. Some statutes list the specific felonies that can be used to establish felony murder. Other statutes simply use language such as "inherently dangerous," "forcible felonies," or "violent felonies." Under either approach, armed robbery would be considered a dangerous felony. Therefore, a killing committed during the commission of armed robbery would be a felony murder. Because malice is assumed, it does not matter that the man hit the pedestrian accidentally. Therefore, **answer A is not correct**.

A crime is not completed until the criminal has reached a place of safety. The thief in this circumstance was not out of danger at the point in which he was driving from the library's parking lot. Because the armed robbery was still being committed as he fled, the man hit the pedestrian during the commission of the felony, not after. *People v. Johnson*, 7 Cal. Rptr. 2d 33 (Cal. App. 1992). For this reason, **answer B is not correct**. Although the pedestrian died as a result of being hit by the thief's car, that fact alone is not sufficient to establish murder. For this reason, **answer D is not the best answer**. A pedestrian who is hit and killed by a carefully driven vehicle, an accident that occurred in the absence of a dangerous crime or felony, would ordinarily not be a victim of murder because the defendant's *mens rea* would be lacking.

82. Liability for the actions of others during the commission of an inherently dangerous felony varies by jurisdiction. On one end of the spectrum, a felon can only be liable if she is the person who directly caused the death, or "pulled the trigger." The rationale underlying this approach is that a person is responsible only for her own acts and that a person should not be held responsible for an act in opposition to her purposes. Under this approach, Sylvia would not be liable for the bystander's death because she did not directly cause his death. Jurisdictions adopting "but for" causation fall at the other end of the spectrum. The rationale underlying this approach is that the felon created the dangerous situation and should be held accountable for any deaths resulting from the situation. Under this approach, Sylvia would be liable for the bystander's death because, but for the crime Sylvia committed and the fact that she was fleeing while a policeman was chasing her at gunpoint, the bystander would not have been killed. Many jurisdictions fall somewhere between these two approaches, using a traditional proximate cause test to determine liability, focusing on the foreseeability of the resulting death. *People v. Matos*, 634 N.E.2d 157 (N.Y. 1994). Under this test, Sylvia likely would be found guilty.

83. Almost certainly, in virtually all jurisdictions, Sylvia will be held criminally responsible for the death of the hostage. Such an action is incredibly dangerous, and foreseeability of great harm to the hostage is quite clear. Most courts would, then, find felony murder here when the felon has taken the additional step of exposing an innocent person to such a high risk. *Jackson v. State*, 408 A.2d 711 (Md. 1979). To be sure, even without a felony murder charge, Sylvia would very likely be found guilty of murder with a determination that her actions were grossly reckless (implied malice).

84. **The best answer is answer A.** In nearly all states, the crime upon which the felony murder rule is predicated must be independent of the felony resulting in homicide.

State v. Miller, 297 N.E.2d 85 (N.Y. 1973). If the felony directly resulting in the homicide were permitted to be the underlying felony, then any assault that resulted in death could be "bumped up" to murder using the assault as the basis for the felony murder. An assault that occurs during a robbery is done with an independent purpose (stealing property), so the robbery can be used as a basis for felony murder. Here, the assault was done with the purpose of physically harming Patrice, so there is no independent purpose for the actions that caused her death. For this reason, the assault cannot be used as the basis for felony murder. Although the assault is a dangerous felony, it is merged with the homicide, so "answer C is incorrect".

Answer B is not correct because the ability to convict on alternate grounds of malice does not preclude the use of the felony murder rule. Often, a person convicted using the felony murder rule could have been convicted by demonstrating malice instead. The felony murder rule provides a shortcut for the prosecution; instead of having to prove malice, which can be difficult, the prosecution must prove only that a dangerous felony occurred and that the homicide occurred during the commission of that felony. Although it is true that "the felony murder rule eliminates the need to demonstrate malice," this statement is not responsive to the question. **Answer D is, therefore, not the best answer**.

85. Felony murder involves a killing that occurs during the commission of a dangerous felony. Because Ronald and Janie were still at the scene of the arson, the killings clearly occurred during the commission of dangerous felony. Jurisdictions differ as to how they approach liability both for killings by co-felons and for killings by third parties. Ronald did not directly commit either murder, so guilt would have to be imputed to him as a party to the crime. Janie would have been guilty of murdering the bystander, so Ronald would be guilty as a co-felon for this foreseeable killing.

Ronald may not be guilty for Janie's death, however, under the felony murder rule. In states adopting one extreme approach, a felon is not liable—under the rule—for killings committed by third parties. *Smith v. Myers*, 261 A.2d 550 (Pa. 1970). Ronald would not be held accountable for the killing of his partner in such states because the police officer was acting in opposition to the purposes of the crime. In states adopting a contrary approach, a felon is responsible for all foreseeable killings that occur during the commission of the felony no matter who directly causes the deaths. *Jackson v. State*, 408 A.2d 711 (Md. 1979). Because it was foreseeable that Ronald, Janie, or another person could have been killed during the arson, Ronald would be guilty of felony murder of Janie in states adopting the foreseeable killings approach, even though neither he nor his co-felon pulled the trigger that caused the bystander's death.

86. **The correct answer is A.** In a felony murder prosecution, the government is relieved of its duty to generally prove a high state of mind as to the killing because of the danger created by the commission of the underlying violent felony. Still, the felony murder theory can only proceed if that underlying violent felony has been proved beyond a reasonable doubt, even if that crime is not separately charged. *People v. Croy*, 710 P.2d 392 (Cal. 1985). Hence, **answers C and D are incorrect**. **Answer B is also incorrect**, as it deals with the harmless error rule, a principle only involved when an error was committed by the trial court.

87. **Answer A is the best answer.** Under the modern law in many jurisdictions, murder is divided into degrees. First degree murder requires the intent to kill and also premeditation and deliberation. *Austin v. United States*, 38 F.2d 129 (D.C. Cir. 1967). Based on Hannibal's statement, a jury could determine that he intended to kill his victims, and that he killed them with deliberation and after premeditation. On this basis, Hannibal can be found guilty of first degree murder.

Second degree murder is a lesser included offense of first degree murder. That is, first degree murder contains all the elements of second degree murder, and also the added elements of premeditation and deliberation. By removing those two elements, second degree murder is defined as an unlawful killing with malice aforethought. **Answer B is not the best answer** because Hannibal, in addition to committing these murders with malice, fulfilled the added elements included in the offense of first degree murder, premeditation and deliberation. For the same reason, **answer C is not the best answer**. Although Hannibal satisfied each of the elements required for a conviction for second degree murder, a conviction for first degree murder is more appropriate because he killed with premeditation and deliberation.

Answer D is not correct. Voluntary manslaughter is murder, but reduced due to the added "heat of passion" element. Hannibal cannot claim to have acted in the heat of passion as it is, by definition, an immediate response to serious provocation. Because Hannibal carefully planned the murders, he cannot be said to have acted in the heat of passion and his killings cannot be viewed as voluntary manslaughter.

88. **Answer A is the best answer.** First degree murder, by statute, often involves the unlawful killing of a person with malice aforethought, plus premeditation and deliberation. Mary planned the murder for over a year, so she had plenty of time to consider and reconsider her actions. Given the circumstances in this case, it appears that Mary acted with malice aforethought (satisfied here by an intent to kill), premeditation, and deliberation. Because the intent to kill, in and of itself, is not sufficient for a conviction of first degree murder, **answer B is not correct.**

Particularly gruesome and heinous homicides are usually first degree murders. The rationale is that the defendant must have had time to consider his/her actions during the course of the murder. For example, one may intend to kill and stab a person all in a few seconds. To kill a person by carving him up into little pieces takes considerably more time. A person who commits such a crime clearly had time to think about what he was doing during the commission of the crime. Nonetheless, not all first degree murders are gruesome or heinous. First degree murder only requires that the defendant have formed an intent to kill and then deliberated and premeditated on it. For this reason, **answer C is not correct**.

Second degree murder is the unlawful killing of a person with malice aforethought (but without premeditation and deliberation). Second degree murder is the "typical" type of murder; most murders fall into this category. Intent to kill is one way of demonstrating the mental state for second degree murder. In this case, Mary had the intent to kill. For that reason, she had the mental state to be convicted of second degree murder. However, because she planned the murder ahead of time, she had the added elements of premeditation and deliberation necessary for a conviction for first degree murder. Although Mary could be convicted of second degree murder, **answer D is not the best answer**. Answer A is the more complete answer, and the best answer applied to these facts, because it includes the elements of both first degree and second degree murder, elements that Mary satisfied.

89. The proposed jury instruction illustrates clearly the great—but unresolved—debate found in courts throughout the United States regarding the evidence necessary to demonstrate the mental state for the crime of first degree murder. Some courts emphasize that the time factor is insignificant. Instead, the real question concerns whether the defendant thoughtfully considered his actions prior to killing. For these courts, the instruction would be proper, as it would demonstrate to the jurors that reflection by the defendant was the important issue, not the time frame for the killing. *Clozza v. State*, 321 S.E.2d 273 (Va. 1984). Other courts, however, take quite a different view. They conclude that allowing a finding of premeditation and deliberation based on actions that took place mere moments apart obscures the distinction between the two degrees of murder. They would require considerably more proof to show true considered decision-making by the defendant in killing the victim. *People v. Guthrie*, 461 S.E.2d 163 (W. Va. 1995).

90. **Answer B is the best answer.** The *corpus delicti* of a crime is the "body of the crime." This phrase is usually referred to when there is a problem demonstrating that a crime has actually occurred, such as when the body of a person suspected to be killed is not recovered. To demonstrate that a death was the result of murder, the prosecution must establish the basic elements of the crime: an unlawful act done with malicious intent that caused the death of a person. All elements of a crime can be proven beyond a reasonable doubt using only circumstantial evidence. Given the circumstantial evidence in this case, including the fact that Juanita purchased a large insurance policy on Bill's life and that Bill has not been heard from since he left for his trip with Juanita, the elements of the crime of murder could be shown in this case, even if Bill's body is never recovered. Hence, **answer D is not correct**.

Answer A is not the best answer because it does not establish an element of the crime of murder. Motive alone is insufficient to prove a causal relationship between a death and a defendant. There must be enough evidence to prove the elements of the crime of murder (*i.e.*, the killing of a person, with malice afore-thought) beyond a reasonable doubt.

In criminal law, the *mens rea* of intent is almost always proven by circumstantial evidence because no one can know for certain what the defendant intended. Generally, the jury considers the evidence and determines that the only reasonable explanation for the defendant's actions is that she intended to do what she did. In the same way, the *actus reus* can also be proven by circumstantial evidence. In this case, the prosecution will show that the only reasonable explanation for Bill's disappearance is that he is dead. Based in part upon such an analysis, Juanita can be convicted of murder. A body is not required to prove beyond a reasonable doubt that a death has occurred if such circumstantial evidence exists. *People v. Scott*, 1 Cal. Rptr. 600 (Cal. App. 1960). Therefore, **answer C is incorrect**.

[3] Manslaughter

91.   Voluntary manslaughter. This crime may be viewed as a murder, but one committed in the "heat of passion." Voluntary manslaughter occurs when there is a sudden provocation that is serious enough that it would cause a reasonable person to act in the same violent way that the defendant did. *State v. Munoz*, 827 P.2d 1303 (N.M. 1992). In such cases, the prosecution will prove all of the elements of murder. While the defendant need not offer any evidence, normally the defense will introduce credible evidence showing that the crime was committed in the heat of passion, as here. The government would be able to demonstrate beyond a reasonable doubt, from his actions, that Joe stabbed Sarah with the intent either to kill her or to inflict great bodily harm to her. Without facts indicating heat of passion and adequate provocation, then, the crime here would be second degree murder. The showing of going "berserk" in response to the argument would, however, likely prove the element necessary for voluntary manslaughter.

92.   In most jurisdictions Joe would now be found guilty of murder rather than voluntary manslaughter. The latter crime requires a showing of an intentional killing done *suddenly* in the heat of passion caused by adequate provocation. The factor of suddenness is taken seriously by most judges. *People v. Wilson*, 278 N.E.2d 473 (Ill. 1972). They are willing to determine that reasonable people might, in the moment, take regrettable actions making them less culpable. If those same people, however, are able to reflect on the situation, the notion of lower culpability vanishes. Suddenness is required for the crime of voluntary manslaughter.

93.   **Answer C is the best answer.** Although the criminal laws generally do not require one to act in aid of another, certain individuals may have a legal duty to take affirmative actions to assist others by virtue of their personal relationships. Under the common law, a duty of care was limited to very few relationships (e.g., parent/child, master/servant). *Commonwealth v. Konz*, 450 A.2d 638 (Pa. 1982). Because Anna was a small child and Tim was her father, Tim was obligated to seek medical attention when his daughter became very ill. **Answer A is incorrect** because it applies the general rules of criminal law without considering the special relationship between Tim and his daughter that creates a duty to act.

Answer B is not correct because it does not accurately explain Tim's motives. Tim put off going to the doctor for financial reasons even when he knew his daughter needed medical attention. To withhold medical assistance for financial reasons exposed Tim's daughter to a substantial risk without reasonable justification. On this basis, Tim exhibited gross recklessness because he knew that keeping Anna at home was putting her in danger.

Voluntary manslaughter has, essentially, the same elements as murder but also "heat of passion," as explained below. **Answer D is not correct** because a lack of financial resources is not a legally adequate provocation. Acts taken in the heat of passion must be done in response to sudden, shocking provocation and must be the sort of response that an ordinary person might make. *People v. Wharton*, 809 P.2d 290 (Cal. 1991). Because no such sudden provocation occurred here, and because most individuals would not respond to financial hardship by refusing to bring their very sick child to the doctor, Tim's actions cannot be seen as arising in the heat of passion.

94. **Answer D is the best answer**, for murder can be based on such extreme risk being consciously taken by a defendant, even without any sort of intentional misconduct. *Commonwealth v. Perry*, 607 N.E.2d 434 (Mass. 1993). With his own observations and the advice from the doctor, Tim may be viewed as having acted with gross recklessness, satisfying the "implied malice" requirement for murder. For that reason, **answers A and B are wrong. Answer C is wrong** because without the information from the doctor it is not likely that a trier of fact would conclude that the risk was sufficiently great as to constitute murder rather than involuntary manslaughter. It should be noted, though, that the distinction between the two crimes is not well defined, and courts have considerable leeway in this area in terms of the proof presented.

95. Involuntary manslaughter is a homicide committed in a reckless fashion. *Commonwealth v. Agnew*, 398 A.2d 209 (Pa. 1979). Jerome hit the man with the intent to kill or harm. The intent does not have to exist far in advance; it may be formed only moments before acting. Jerome clearly stated that his intent was to kill the man; therefore, he is not guilty of involuntary manslaughter.

Voluntary manslaughter is an intentional killing done in the heat of passion, in response to a sudden adequate provocation. At common law, words alone were not enough to constitute adequate provocation in order to reduce murder to voluntary manslaughter. *People v. Castro*, 592 P.2d 185 (N.M. 1979). Some states still follow this rule. In those jurisdictions, Jerome would be guilty of murder. He would not be allowed to assert that the act was done in the heat of passion because as a matter of law, words could not have provoked a reasonable person to kill. Jerome would have had to walk in on his wife and the man together or have had some sort of proof other than mere words to be able to claim that the murder was done in the heat of passion in response to adequate provocation.

Other states find that words alone may be sufficient to provoke a person to kill. In most of those jurisdictions that allow words alone, the courts consider whether or not there is sufficient evidence to show that a reasonable person would have been incited to kill in a hot-blooded passion. The evidence may be acts, acts and words, or words alone. In those jurisdictions, the murder could be reduced to a conviction of voluntary manslaughter. *Girouard v. State*, 583 A.2d 718 (Md. 1991).

96. **B is the best answer.** Involuntary manslaughter is an unlawful killing resulting from a reckless disregard for human life. The defendant must be aware of the risk, as Patrick was here. The degree of risk is less than that required for murder, defined as great or gross recklessness. There are no clear lines, but courts have defined recklessness in many different ways such as disregard for human life, an indifference to consequences, or a taking of a risk that likely could result in *serious* harm or death.

In most states, vehicular homicide resulting from some physical ailment or defect (e.g., drowsiness or vertigo caused by medication or alcohol; epilepsy) is usually involuntary manslaughter. Although people are aware of the risks involved, they do not expect it to happen to them. For the act to be successfully prosecuted as murder, it must be a *grossly* reckless act so likely to result in serious harm or death that the defendant virtually intended that result. Driving under the influence of medication does not rise to this level of risk; therefore, **answer A is not the best answer.**

Common tort negligence is based on the notion that a reasonable person would have known of the risk. Here the defendant was warned multiple times and had noticed how drowsy he became while taking the medicine. His later actions show a conscious disregard for safety and constitute reckless endangerment of the lives of others. Patrick's behavior far exceeds mere negligence, so **answer C is not the best answer.**

Although it may not have been likely that the driver of the other car would be killed at such low speeds, Patrick knew that driving a car in his condition could result in the death of himself or another driver. The exact scenario that results in death does not have to be foreseeable. It is enough that it was foreseeable that Patrick's driving was likely to result in serious injury or death. Therefore, **answer D is not the best answer**.

[D] Kidnapping

97. **The best answer is B.** Kidnapping consists of the unlawful confinement or removal of another, without consent, from that person's location of choice. *People v. Gonzalez*, 603 N.E. 2d 938 (N.Y. 1992). Even a short distance away is sufficient to constitute a kidnapping, so **answer C is wrong**. *People v. Shadden*, 112 Cal. Rptr. 2d 826 (Cal. App. 2001). **Answer A is not correct**, for kidnapping only occurs if there is some confinement or movement against the will of the victim. The crime can be committed with the use of force, or the threatened use of force. Therefore, **answer D is also not correct**.

98. The **best answer is A,** as the force or threat of force need not be directed to any specific person for the crime of kidnapping to occur. *State v. Elenes-Rocha*, 1997 Wash. App. Lexis 342 (Wash. App. 1997). **Answer C, then, is incorrect. Answer B is not right**, as some force or threat of force is normally needed to satisfy the elements of the crime of kidnapping. Thus, **answer D is also not right.**

99. **The best answer is C.** The time frame for the confinement is irrelevant, so long as the defendant is moved against his will, as in this case. *United States v. Hernandez-Montoya*, 2002 U.S. App. Lexis 8637 (4ᵗʰ Cir. 2002). **Answer A, thus, is incorrect, as is answer B,** for the crime never requires any physical injury to be sustained by the victim. And, as indicated above, the crime is complete with the confinement or movement, not with the threat. Hence, **answer "D" is also incorrect.**

100. Yes, the kidnapping was complete very soon after Professor Hortense remained in the room against her will. While Taylor will raise a number of fairly serious points

in response to the prosecution, none will succeed. It is true that the professor was forced to remain in the room rather that required to move to another location. Kidnapping, however, involves either the removal of the victim or her confinement. Moreover, the fact that the confinement took place in a public area is of no import. The key to the crime is that the defendant has forced the victim to move, or not move, against her will. Finally, the mere fact that the confinement was limited to a ten-minute period does not matter. Essentially, any period of unlawful movement or confinement is sufficient for the purpose of the crime of kidnapping. While some modern statutes have degrees of the crime, linked to the time of the movement/ confinement, these laws do not usually redefine the crime; they simply alter the punishment depending on the seriousness of the offense.

[E] Robbery

101. **The correct answer is B.** In order to meet the requirements for a robbery, the defendant must take another's property from that person by violence or intimidation. *State v. Felix*, 737 P.2d 393 (Az. App. 1986). Regardless of whether the defendant would have been able to harm the victim, if the victim was in fact intimidated, then that element has been met. Therefore, **answers C and D are incorrect**. Robbery thus requires more than just a larceny, and is punishable by lengthier sentences. **Answer A is incorrect** for this reason. Robbery is considered more serious than larceny because it is a crime against both property and person, as it involves the use or threat of violence against the victim.

102. Paul will not be found guilty of robbery. Robbery is a crime against the person, not simply a property offense. As such, it requires a showing of force or threat of force directed against a victim. Because of this element, the punishment for robbery is normally considerably greater than for theft offenses. A pickpocket generally does not commit the crime of robbery, for his skill is in taking the property without notice, as opposed to using or threatening to use force against the victim.

[F] Sex Offenses

103. **Answer C is the best answer.** At common law, and in most statutes today, the crime of rape consists of sexual intercourse by force or threat of force with no consent by the victim. The forced entry of Lance inside Sheena's body, without any indication of approval by Sheena would be sufficient to show no consent by her to the act. *Commonwealth v. Caracciola*, 569 N.E. 2d 774 (Mass. 1991). **Answer D is wrong**, because the consent need not be express so long as some indication is given that the consent is voluntary and understood by both parties.

In a situation such as this, silence of the victim typically is insufficient to show consent and some indication of assent must be demonstrated. Thus, **answer B is incorrect. Answer A is also incorrect**, as it is not enough for the defendant to show that he did not realize there was a lack of approval of the act. Rather, the prosecution will succeed if the government shows that the victim did not consent, as is the case here.

104. At common law, many states required the specific threat or use of force to be made before conviction for the crime of rape would be allowed. That is no longer the law in most jurisdictions. The forced entry of Lance inside Sheena's body—under circumstances that would cause any reasonable person to be terrified—constitutes the use of force in most jurisdictions. The sheer size difference between the parties, the awakening of the victim to see the defendant without clothes, and the lack of communication could, taken together, constitute the key element of the crime, the use of force. *People v. Iniguez*, 872 P. 2d 1183 (Cal. 1994).

105. **Answer A is the best answer.** Under the common law, and still in most states, rape requires the use of physical force or threat of force resulting in serious bodily harm to compel the victim to have sex. Courts and legislatures still, generally, find that threats other than those likely to result in serious bodily harm are insufficient for the crime. The threat of losing a job or a contract, or even a scholarship, would be insufficient to show force or lack of consent. Although the government would argue that Alice was compelled by Bob's threat, most courts would find his actions to fall outside the statutory prohibition. *State v. Thompson*, 792 P. 2d 1103 (Mon. 1990). For this reason, **answer C is wrong.**

While rape is viewed as a violent crime, the threatened use of actual force would be a sufficient basis for the successful prosecution of the offense even without an expression of protest, as noted above. Hence, **answer B is not the best answer. Answer D is wrong** because Alice seemed not to consent. The problem here is not one of consent, but rather no showing of use of force.

106. **Answer B is the best answer.** The traditional approach to "statutory rape" was that sex with a child under the age of consent (set by law) was rape, regardless of whether the child had consented or not. The view was that the minor could not make an informed decision, and therefore could not consent to sex. The modern approach now permits a defense of reasonable mistake in the context of "statutory rape" in which the child has consented and is near the age of consent. The likelihood that such a defense will be successful, however, depends largely upon the child's age. The younger the child, the less likely courts will accept the defense of reasonable mistake. In such cases, the offense approaches strict liability on this matter. In these circumstances, Brandon had good reason to believe that Cate was an adult, so he may be able to rely upon a defense of reasonable mistake to the crime of rape. *People v. Hernandez*, 393 P. 2d 673 (Cal. 1964).

Cate did seemingly agree to the sexual intercourse. When a child is under the statutorily defined age of consent, the law makes a presumption that the girl could not make an informed decision and could not legally consent to sex. Thus, absent a defense of reasonable mistake, consent of a minor to the sex act is irrelevant. For example, if Cate had been 12 instead of 17, a court would probably not accept such a defense from Brandon and whether or not Cate consented to the sex would be irrelevant. Because the important inquiry raised by this question is whether a court would allow a defense of reasonable mistake, not whether Cate consented to the sex act, **answer A is incorrect.**

Cate is under the age of consent. Legally, she is presumed to be incapable of consenting to sex. At common law, Brandon would have been guilty of rape; the age of consent was a "bright line" limit under which a child could not consent to sex. As the modern approach would allow Brandon the defense of a reasonable mistake, he might not be guilty of rape in jurisdictions following this approach. Because answer "C" restates the common law rule and does not take into account recent modifications to that approach, **answer C is not the best answer. Answer D is also not the best answer**, for Brandon had the requisite state of mind. Rape is unusual in that the *mens rea* for the defendant is, for all practical purposes, merely the intent to have sexual intercourse (not the intent to commit rape). Here Brandon intended to have sexual intercourse. However, given the extenuating circumstances (Brandon's reasonable belief that Cate was "of age" and that sex with her was legal), he may have a defense of reasonable mistake.

107. **The best answer is answer C.** While at common law husbands, as a matter of law, could not be found guilty of raping their wives, most jurisdictions today reject that broad ban. *People v. Liberta*, 474 N.E. 2d 567, *cert. denied*, 417 U.S. 1020 (N.Y. 1984). Hence, **answer A is wrong** today.

Throwing the victim onto the bed and then having intercourse with her could certainly be sufficient evidence to demonstrate the use of force, for the purpose of the crime of rape, so that **answer B is not correct. Answer D also is not correct**, as the marital status may be relevant to the prosecution. That is, while the broad ban on marital rape has been eliminated in most jurisdictions, many states do look to the marital relationship as being of significance in determining if a crime has been committed. In some states, there is only a crime if the parties are living apart, while in other states there is a specific time for reporting sexual assaults by marital partners.

108. It depends. For most of our history, the crime was viewed as being committed by a male against a female. Under a traditional common law view of the crime of rape, a man could not be found guilty of raping another man. Even today, some jurisdictions have rape statutes that are gender specific, limited to sexual assaults by men against women. Increasingly, however, such statutes are gender neutral so that a man could be found guilty of raping another man. Typically, these statutes describe various kinds of sexual assaults, not simply those involving vaginal entry, and speak in terms of *persons* being victims and being perpetrators. *People v. Liberta*, 474 N.E. 2d 567, *cert. denied*, 417 U.S. 1020 (N.Y. 1984).

109. The fornication crime, dating back hundreds of years, makes sexual intercourse between unmarried people illegal. Under the traditional common law view, then, answer C would be correct. **Answer C is the wrong answer**, however, because most jurisdictions today have either repealed or overturned such laws. **Answer B, therefore, is the correct answer.**

Answer A is not the correct answer, as there is no clear, definitive ruling that fornication laws are unconstitutional, though certainly several courts have so held. **Answer D is wrong**, as the search here was conducted pursuant to a valid warrant. As a result, there would not be any constitutional violation as indicated by the facts.

110. **Answer C is the best answer.** For a conviction of involuntary manslaughter, there must be a causal relationship between the illegal act and the death. *Commonwealth v. Atencio,* 189 N.E.2d 223 (Mass. 1963). James did not drown as a result of fishing in a location where it was illegal to fish. James fell overboard and drowned as a result of his intoxication. If James had been on another part of the lake, he would still have drowned, so his proximity to the dam was unrelated to his drowning. Therefore, the violation is not a "but for" cause of the drowning.

Answer A is not correct because violating the rule against fishing near the dam was not the cause of James' death. Peter would be responsible if the drowning had occurred due to turbulence caused by the spillway opening, which is the reason that the warning signs are posted. In that case, Peter would be liable because he was in control of the boat and had insisted on fishing in an unsafe location. For that reason, **answer B is also not the best answer**. James is responsible for his own actions, including drinking excessively while on the lake. Had James fallen overboard as a result of turbulence when the spillway was opened, Peter might have been responsible. **Answer D is not the best answer,** however, because the tort defense of assumption of the risk does not exist in the criminal law. Under some circumstances a person may be criminally liable for the knowing—but foolish—actions of another. *Commonwealth v. Feinberg,* 253 A.2d 636 (Pa. 1969).

111. **Answer C is the best answer.** A person is held responsible for an intervening cause of death only if that cause is foreseeable. Although tying Steve up and leaving him for a few hours put Steve at risk, a reasonable person would not expect it to result in this type of death or serious bodily injury. Dying from a rattlesnake bite in Nebraska or Minnesota is not commonplace. Finding rattlesnakes indoors is even less common. Anne had no reason to expect that a rattlesnake would be in the building, so Steve's death was not foreseeable.

Answer A is not the best answer because involuntary manslaughter requires more than simply negligent behavior. To be guilty of involuntary manslaughter, Anne's actions must be reckless, seriously endangering the safety of another person. Gross recklessness is behavior that shows a blatant disregard for human life. Reckless behavior may cause serious injury; gross recklessness will likely cause serious injury or even death. **Answer B is not the best answer** because Anne's tying a person up in a vacant office building in that part of the country would not normally result in serious bodily injury or death. If Anne had tied up Steve in an abandoned desert warehouse in the southwest, she could be guilty of involuntary manslaughter because the probability of getting bit by a rattlesnake there would be considerably higher. Under those circumstances, it might be foreseeable that a venomous snake in a vacant building would bite Steve. Involuntary manslaughter is an unlawful death that results from reckless behavior. **Answer D is not the best answer** because Anne did not have to intend to harm Steve to be guilty of involuntary manslaughter. Intent to harm is not an element of involuntary manslaughter.

112.   Yes, Anne would now likely be held for the manslaughter charge. While death in certain parts of the country from a rattlesnake bite may not be very likely, death from a heart attack is quite foreseeable in the situation. Tying someone up and leaving him alone with the knowledge that he might never be found is truly reckless behavior likely to result in some sort of serious injury such as that resulting from a heart attack. The key issue is foreseeability, and that issue is resolved on a case by case basis, being quite fact specific. *People v. Foster*, 396 N.E.2d 246 (Ohio 1979).

113.   **Answer A is the best answer.** While Flo's own action directly contributed to her death, it was the brutal beating by Jessie that caused Flo to be in the hospital and to receive the message as to her permanent disfigurement. Under these extreme circumstances, though Jessie may not have intended the death, it was foreseeable. *Brackett v. Peters*, 11 F.3d 78 (7th Cir. 1993). **Answer B is wrong** because foreseeability is required for criminal responsibility with such an interviewing event.

While Flo's action in pulling out the tube in fact caused her death, in the situation described above, such action by the victim does not relieve the defendant of criminal responsibility. The death is still deemed foreseeable. Hence, **answer C is not correct**. For the same reason, **answer D is not correct**. Even intervening negligence in such a situation will not break the chain of causation. The defendant is criminally responsible because her brutal behavior created an extremely high-risk situation. *James v. State*, 366 So.2d 1155 (Ala. 1979).

[A] Self-Defense

114.   **Answer C is the best answer.** Under the general rule of self-defense, a person can use whatever non-lethal force appears to be reasonably necessary to prevent immediate harm to herself. With limited exceptions, an individual cannot use deadly force in self-defense. However, a killing committed by a defendant in self-defense is justified under the law if she reasonably believed that: (1) she was in imminent danger at the time she took an action; and (2) deadly force was necessary in response to the perceived danger. *People v. Griffiths*, 610 P.2d 522 (Idaho 1980). Under the circumstances, Bonny could have reasonably believed that she was in imminent danger of serious bodily injury and that the shot she fired was necessary to respond to the threat posed. Thus, she can argue that her actions should be protected as made in self-defense. The jury should receive instructions on self-defense in this case.

        Answer A is not the best answer because an endangered person does not have to wait until an aggressor has already acted in any specific aggressive manner before the person is entitled, under the law, to defend herself. So long as Bonnie reasonably believed both that she was in imminent danger at the time she shot the man and that deadly force was necessary in response to this danger, the jury should be able to consider whether Bonnie's actions should be deemed self-defense.

        With the facts presented, it is not clear that Bonny could have safely escaped in her car. Under the law, a person only has a duty to retreat before using deadly force in one's own defense if it is clear that such an escape can be made without incurring bodily harm. Therefore, **answer B is incorrect**. **Answer D is not the best answer** because it only addresses a single element of self-defense. Bonny's subjective belief that she was in imminent danger would not be sufficient for her actions to be deemed self-defense under the law. In presenting a self-defense claim, the defendant's belief is based principally upon an objective, rather than a subjective, standard. In order to get the benefit of this defense, a reasonable person in her circumstances must have believed that she was in imminent danger and that her actions were necessary to respond to this apparent danger.

115.   Self-defense is permitted when: (1) a person believes that force is needed to prevent harm to one's self; (2) that belief is reasonable; (3) the person believes that the amount of force used is necessary; and (4) that belief is reasonable. The belief that the use of force is necessary and that the amount of force used is necessary only has to be reasonable, it does not have to be correct in fact. Mistake is permitted. For this reason, the stranger's actual intentions do not affect the outcome. Therefore, if Bonny was justified (under a reasonable person standard) in using deadly force against the man, the fact that she was not actually in danger does not change the result. *People v. Humphrey*, 56 Cal. Rptr. 2d 142 (Cal. 1996).

116.   **Answer B is the best answer.** In order to respond to another person with deadly force, one must reasonably believe that he is faced with imminent danger of serious bodily injury or death and that deadly force is necessary to respond to the threat posed. Under these facts, the hiker was faced with a threat, but not with serious bodily injury or death. Given their relative sizes and the use of a knife as opposed to a gun, a reasonable person would have seen that he could have disarmed Bonny, threatened her with the gun, or otherwise avoided killing her. *People v. Goetz,* 497 N.E.2d 41 (N.Y. 1986). Because a person is not entitled to rely upon self-defense in the use of deadly force if he could reasonably and safely have avoided deadly force, the hiker could not rely upon such a defense under these facts.

   Answer A is not correct because deadly force may sometimes be used in self-defense. Normally, deadly force can only be used to prevent apparent serious bodily injury or death, from which the person could not safely escape. Given the circumstances in this scenario, however, the hiker could not rely upon the defense of self in his use of deadly force. **Answer D is not the best answer** because the stranger's subjective beliefs are not sufficient to warrant the use of deadly force. In order to rely upon the defense of self-defense, the hiker's belief in the apparent imminent danger and his belief that the amount of force he used was necessary both must be objectively reasonable. **Answer C is not correct.** Although the use of a knife is often considered an escalation to the use of deadly force, other factors such as the relative size of the parties and other weapons must be considered in determining the nature of the threat posed and the ability of the person threatened to safely escape. Additional factors that may be relevant in this consideration are the age and health of the parties, the presence of multiple assailants, or a past history of violence between the parties. *State v. Marks,* 602 P.2d 1344 (Kan. 1979). Because the threatened use of a knife does not automatically pose a threat of deadly force, that threat does not necessarily justify the use of deadly force under a theory of self-defense.

117.   **Answer C is the best answer.** Although Matthew was the aggressor, Donald would only have a right to use force in response if such force would be necessary to prevent further bodily harm. If a person generally could retreat from a violent situation without experiencing physical harm, then the use of force is not necessary and the person cannot rely upon an argument of self-defense in many states. Donald could have retreated (either before or after Matthew's shove) without resorting to violence. The exception to this retreat rule, however, is when the altercation occurs in the defendant's own home. *State v. Garland,* 694 A.2d 564 (N.J. 1997). For this reason, **answer B is not the best answer. Answer A is not the best answer**. An act need not be extremely violent in order to make a person an aggressor. Matthew's shove, which appeared designed to provoke a physical confrontation, was more than enough to make Matthew the aggressor. **Answer D is incorrect**. The law does not permit unrestricted "tit-for-tat" behaviors. Although one may act in self-defense when he reasonably believes that force is necessary to avoid bodily harm, the law does not protect a person who has used force when an alternative to the use of force was available. The fact that a person has been attacked does not necessarily protect his actions, taken in response, as self-defense.

118. **Answer A is the best answer.** Although resistance to unlawful arrests was once considered acceptable, over half of the states have now made it illegal to resist an arrest, whether lawful or unlawful. *People v. Valentine*, 935 P.2d 1294 (Wash. 1997). Underlying this trend are the premises that violence, particularly against peace officers, is not the best way to resolve conflicts and citizens should rely on the modern criminal justice system to protect their rights. Thus **answer C is incorrect**.

Answer B is not the best answer because it does not comport with the facts described. In these circumstances, the officers initiated the conflict when they confronted Jen. Thus, if the two individuals were not police officers, Jen could likely rely upon self-defense as a justification for her actions. This conflict, however, arose from an attempted arrest by police officers. For this reason, the law in most jurisdictions would not allow Jen to resist at all. **Answer D is not the best answer** because it fails to take into account the fact that the individuals Jen encountered were police officers who were trying to question and then arrest her. Of course, the fact that Jen was outnumbered would normally be relevant to a claim of self-defense (*e.g.*, to examine whether Jen could have reasonably retreated from the situation and the extent of the threat posed).

119. **Answer B is the best answer.** The person who starts a fight by acting as the aggressor cannot claim self-defense. In addition, a person is barred from the justification of self-defense if he escalates the amount of force being used. In this scenario, Bruce began a shoving match. Ryan's use of a weapon increased the amount of harm that was likely to result from the altercation. Thus, he escalated the conflict and as such Ryan is barred from a claim of self-defense. *People v. Marks*, 602 P.2d 1344 (Kan. 1979). **Answer A is thus incorrect.**

Although Bruce started the fight, Ryan became the aggressor when he pulled a knife. A defendant may only use a lawful amount of force in self-defense. Such a lawful amount of force is only that level of force that reasonably appears necessary to prevent harm to one's person. Any force beyond that level is deemed unlawful force. In using unlawful force, a person (even a person who was initially a victim) becomes the aggressor. In this case, Ryan's use of the knife was an unlawful response to Bruce's shove because that level of force was not required to avoid the harm Bruce might have caused. Hence, **answer C is not correct**.

In a fight between two individuals, neither of whom is using a weapon, the introduction of a deadly weapon generally constitutes an unlawful escalation. Although the knife in this case did not cause any serious injuries to Bruce, Ryan's use of the knife was unlawful. Ryan's unlawful use of force transformed him into the aggressor in the fight, which deprived him of a right to claim self-defense, regardless of how much harm he actually caused with the knife. Because the actual level of harm caused to Bruce is irrelevant to whether Ryan can claim self-defense, **answer D is not correct**.

120. **Answer C is the best answer.** Lola had a great deal of evidence demonstrating that she had been the victim of an abusive spouse for many years. Battered spouses may be able to predict violent outbursts more accurately than a casual observer.

Therefore, Lola knew that Mel was going to become extremely violent the night he died, even though he had not yet made any threats against Lola. Most states now allow evidence of battered spouse syndrome in circumstances in which the battered spouse suffers from an inability to remove him/herself from an abusive relationship. The syndrome has been used in the self-defense context to show that a battered spouse must act before the abusive spouse's action become life-threatening. *Bechtel v. State*, 840 P.2d 1 (Okla. App. 1992). The battered spouse syndrome may be seen as a relaxation of the traditional requirement, for a claim of self-defense, that the harm defended against must be imminent. Therefore, **answer B is not the best answer**.

One is almost never required to retreat from one's own home. Although the issue is more complicated when the assailant lives in the same place as the victim, most states would not require Lola to leave her home. In addition, because Lola may be able to present a self-defense claim relying upon battered spouse syndrome, **answer A is not correct. Answer D is not the best answer** because prior incidents do not automatically justify the use of deadly force. Prior violent behavior may, however, be used to show the reasonableness of a defendant's fear of serious bodily injury. Particularly, in the case of battered spouse syndrome, courts often allow the use of deadly force after prior violent behavior with the expectation that violent behavior will occur again immediately.

[B]   Defense of Others

121.   **Answer C is the best answer.** Richard could attack the man if Richard used a necessary amount of force based upon a reasonable belief that the man posed a serious threat to the child. The approach used in most states today allows defenders to use reasonable force to defend someone whom they reasonably believe is being unlawfully attacked. In this case, Richard need only reasonably believe that force is necessary to protect the child in order to rely upon a claim of defense of others. *People v. Pendley*, 593 P.2d 755 (N.M. 1979). **Answer A is not the best answer** because it reflects the approach embodied in an old rule that is no longer used in most states. The old rule restricted the use of force in defense of others to those with whom the defender had a special relationship (e.g., parent and child, employer and employee). Unlike that old approach, the modern, majority view encourages strangers and friends to assist one another when they are threatened with harm.

Answer B is not correct because bystanders are not required to wait and gather all of the facts before assisting someone who appears to be in immediate danger of bodily harm. Instead, one may act on behalf of another so long as he has a reasonable belief that the person being assisted is in immediate danger of unlawful, bodily harm. **Answer D is the wrong answer** because it reflects an approach no longer incorporated into most modern statutes. The older rule, known as the "alter ego" view, discouraged strangers from interfering with one another by punishing those who acted based upon a misunderstanding of the situation. Under the old law, Richard would only be justified to act on the child's behalf if the child would be permitted to use the same amount of force in self-defense. The test today, however, is whether the individual acted reasonably under the circumstances.

122. **Answer A is the best answer.** Richard acted based on a reasonable belief that the man posed a serious threat to the child. Under the modern, majority view, mistakes are permitted. This approach encourages people to come to the aid of others by not punishing those who act out of an intent to help someone in need, even if all of the facts relating to the situation are not uncovered before action is taken. The result would be the same whether the man was actually trying to abduct the child or whether he was trying to prevent the abduction of his child, so long as it reasonably appeared to be an abduction. **Answer C therefore is wrong**.

   Answer B is incorrect because Richard was justified in acting under the modern approach in both sets of circumstances. Under the old approach, this answer would be correct because Richard did not have a special, protected relationship with the child. **Answer D is not the best answer** because the possibility raised there is not relevant to the question asked. As noted above, the old approach to defense of others (also known as the "alter ego" rule) is no longer used in most states.

123. Under the "alter ego" rule discussed above, the customer's actions would not be justified. Using the "alter ego" rule, the customer would only be justified to act in defense of Stephan if Stephan would be permitted to use the same amount of force in self-defense. Stephan would not be allowed to resist the arrest by the security guard because the arrest, in response to Stephan's shoplifting, was lawful. Therefore, the customer would not be justified in defending Stephan. *State v. Fair*, 211 A.2d 359 (N.J. 1965). This is the main argument in favor of the "alter ego" rule; it protects law enforcement from well-meaning, but misguided, members of the public.

   With the modern, majority rule, the customer's actions would be permitted. This approach allows one to act on behalf of another if he reasonably believes that the amount of force is necessary to prevent bodily harm. The customer saw Stephan being attacked by another man and reasonably thought that force was necessary to stop this apparent attack. Although the customer was mistaken about the situation, he was justified in using force to prevent further bodily harm to Stephan. The modern approach encourages bystanders to act on behalf of others, and allows mistakes so long as a reasonable person would have acted as the defender did.

[C] Defense of Property

124. **Answer B is the best answer.** Deadly force is never justified merely for the protection of personal property. A reasonable amount of force may be used to prevent the theft of property. However, the law provides that deadly force used to stop the theft of property is not reasonable. *Commonwealth v. Emmons*, 43 A.2d 568 (Pa. 1945). Almost any other type of force, short of deadly force, used to prevent the theft of property might be reasonable. As human life is valued higher than any amount of property, even a fancy car, **answer D is not the best answer.**

   Answer A is the wrong answer. As explained above, the use of deadly force is not a reasonable amount of force to use in defense of property. The use of a firearm is considered deadly force, even in circumstances in which the person targeted does not die. Moreover, Melissa's actions could not be defended as self-defense where deadly force might be allowed. Although answer C contains a correct statement of the law, this statement is incomplete. The use of force is permitted to prevent or stop the imminent theft of property, provided that the amount of force is reasonable. Because the use of deadly force to protect personal property alone is not reasonable, **answer C is incorrect.**

125.   **Answer D is the best answer.** Most states provide that one may use deadly force in a home invasion situation if he believes that the criminal is attempting to commit a serious crime, such force is necessary to prevent the offense, and the use of non-deadly force to prevent the crime would expose the defendant or another innocent person to substantial risk of serious bodily injury. New York Penal Law § 35.20. Seeing the man coming up the stairs toward his family, Burt could reasonably have believed that the man was a danger, force was necessary to stop him, and the use of non-deadly force would have put Burt or his family at great risk.

Most states allow the use of deadly force to prevent crimes in one's home. Under this approach, one does not have to permit a thief to take violent action in order to avoid a killing. For this reason, **answer A is not the best answer**.

Answer B is not the correct answer. Burt did not have to attempt non-deadly means to stop the man if Burt believed reasonably that to do so would endanger his family. If Burt thought that the use of non-deadly force would endanger him or his family, he was not under an obligation to use such force as an alternative to deadly force. **Answer C is wrong** because it is too general. The law does not permit one to use deadly force whenever a dwelling is burglarized. The defendant must actually believe that the use of such force is necessary to prevent serious harm to himself or to another innocent person before the use of deadly force can be justified.

[D] Duress

126.   The elements of duress are: (1) another person threatens serious bodily harm or death to the defendant or a third person; (2) the defendant reasonably believes that the threat is real; (3) the threat is imminent at the time the crime is committed; (4) no reasonable escape exists; and (5) the defendant is blameless for the instigation of the threat. The statutory defense of duress is generally similar to the common law defense of duress, but may vary, from one jurisdiction to another, in the application of each element. In order for Henrico to rely upon the defense of duress, each of the defense's criteria must be satisfied for each of the crimes with which he is charged.

Henrico may properly assert the defense of duress for the traffic violations he committed. Henrico assumed that the man pointing the gun at his girlfriend was a threat to shoot her. In this case, Henrico reasonably believed that the threat of serious bodily harm was real and that the threat was imminent. Although Henrico might have been able to escape from the car, his girlfriend would likely have been killed. Under the law, Henrico was not required to flee and to allow his girlfriend to be killed, when compliance with the stranger's requests could have preserved both of their lives. Finally, Henrico had not done anything to provoke or create the threat of the gunman.

127. The defense of duress for the murder of the woman will fail. Duress is never a defense to a purposeful killing. *People v. Dittis*, 483 N.W.2d 94, 95 (Mich. App. 1987). In some states where duress has been codified, duress may be used as a mitigating factor to reduce the penalty for the murder or even to drop the crime charged from murder to manslaughter, but it is not a full defense.

128. **Answer B is the best answer.** Under the law, threats of economic reprisals, property damage, damage to one's reputation, and even minor injuries do not justify committing a criminal act. *State v. Verrechia*, 766 A.2d 377 (R.I. 2001). A person may only act under duress when a threat of serious bodily injury or death has been made against him or a third person. Tad was only threatened with the loss of his job—an economic hardship—so he may not use the defense of duress.

One of the elements of a defense of duress is that the threat must be imminent. If Daphne's threat were imminent, that fact would weigh in *favor* of Tad's ability to use the defense. **Answer A is incorrect** because it is a misstatement of an element of duress. Here, Daphne probably could not have immediately implemented her threat. Tad would have had time to consult with Daphne's superiors, an attorney, or law enforcement officers. This answer would be correct if it began "No, as the threat was NOT imminent."

Because Daphne was his boss, Tad reasonably believed that her threat was genuine. That the person being threatened reasonably believes that the threat is real and credible is only one of the elements of duress. **Answer C is not the best answer** because the other elements of the defense (such as imminence and threat of deadly force) are not satisfied. Although one element of the defense of duress is that the person did not create or contribute to the creation of the coercive situation (which would be satisfied in this case because Tad did not provoke Daphne's actions), **answer D is not the best answer** because the other elements of the defense of duress are not satisfied. For example, one may not use the defense of duress if there is a reasonable escape from the threat other than to comply with the demands. Tad could have spoken to Daphne's superiors, probably kept his job, and not complied with her demands. In addition, as explained above, the nature of the threat would not warrant a defense of duress.

[E] Necessity

129. **Answer C is the best answer.** The defense of necessity allows one to violate laws for reasons of social policy. When obeying the law would result in greater harm than that created by the violation of the laws, one may claim the defense of necessity. *Allison v. City of Birmingham*, 580 So.2d 1377 (Ala. Cr. App. 1991). The bodily injury that would have resulted from obeying the laws against trespass, theft, etc., far outweighs the harm created when Gerald used the shelter and supplies. A person may not use the defense of necessity when he has created the problematic

situation. Because Gerald had no reason to expect a winter storm, his lack of preparation did not cause his predicament. Therefore, **answer A is not the best answer**. Note: Had Gerald gone camping in the height of winter when a particularly bad storm was predicted, he might have been precluded from relying upon the defense of necessity. Even in such circumstances, however, the balance between the value of life, as compared to the harm caused by Gerald's irresponsible behavior, could possibly still enable Gerald to rely upon the defense of necessity.

Answer B is not the best answer because the defense of necessity may be used whenever there is the possibility that a violation of the law will result in a lesser harm than if the law is obeyed. Necessity is not limited to life and death situations. The defense of necessity exists to achieve a just result. Most cases of necessity involve a serious harm that would result from obeying the law, but such a result need not rise to the level of involving a choice between life and death. Gerald may claim necessity when the predicament he faced involved a choice between bodily injury and harm to property. In virtually all cases, the interest in human health and safety will outweigh property concerns in a determination of whether individuals can rely upon the defense of necessity. **Answer D is not the best answer** because it is too extreme. A person faced with a situation involving a choice between preserving human safety and a property interest may almost always choose human health and safety and the law will protect that choice by enabling the person to rely upon the defense of necessity. However, a person cannot do anything and everything necessary to preserve one's own life. For example, a person cannot choose to cause serious bodily harm or death to another in order to preserve one's own life.

130.   **Answer A is the best answer.** Financial necessity is generally not a defense to any crime. Necessity is a defense based on social policy. The violation of a law is presumed to result in a greater harm than any harm that could be created by economic hardship. In addition, most instances of economic hardship will have some sort of legal remedy. One may not claim necessity when there is a way to lawfully avoid the harm. *United States v. Talbott*, 78 F.3d 1183 (7th Cir. 1996). **Answer B is incorrect** and is a red herring. Regardless of whether Immanuel was charged in a state following the common law or a modern statute, he could not rely upon the defense of necessity for forging a check to pay a mortgage payment because of dire financial circumstances.

Although necessity is a defense based on social policy, it is designed to prevent injustice resulting from the application of the law. One may not use the defense of necessity in a situation where the legislature has already weighed the harms and decided against the criminal act. Foreclosure is a recognized financial tool. Although legislation may indicate a preference for home ownership, the law also clearly indicates that foreclosure is an acceptable remedy for the failure to make mortgage payments. The societal harm caused by fraud outweighs Immanuel's personal gain from sending a forged check. For this reason, **answer C is not the best answer**. Whether Immanuel was able to pay the bill a week, a month, or even a day later, does not address the balancing of "evils" that the necessity defense requires. The defense of necessity is permitted when the harm resulting from obeying the law would cause a greater harm than breaking the law. Fraud disrupts many societal institutions. Immanuel's short-term personal gain does not outweigh the social harm created by fraud. Immanuel's efforts to lessen the harm of his actions do not excuse him, so **answer D is not the best answer**.

131. **Answer B is the best answer.** One is not excused from criminal acts on the basis of necessity when a lawful option is available. *United States v. Haynes*, 143 F.3d 1089 (7th Cir. 1998). Although speaking to the prison officials would probably not have been helpful, Charlene could have written to the head of the department of corrections, to legislators, or even to the press. In addition, Charlene could have raised her claims in the judicial system by filing a legal action. Because Charlene could have pursued these legal options, she cannot rely upon necessity as a defense to the criminal acts.

    Answer A is not the best answer. The United States Supreme Court has indicated, in *United States v. Bailey*, 444 U.S. 394 (1980), that a prisoner may be excused from escaping from prison if certain criteria are met. State courts have also held, generally in *dicta*, that prisoners do not have to accept egregious treatment. They have also held that the avoided harm must be very extreme and clearly imminent, such as escaping from a beating or a prison fire. As indicated above, prisoners facing less imminent and egregious harms have other avenues to pursue.

    Although states have taken a variety of approaches, they generally agree that a prisoner may escape out of necessity if the prison is on fire or she is directly threatened. Although a prisoner has a right to preserve her own life, the circumstances in which courts have allowed a defense of necessity for escape are extremely narrow. Charlene was not in such a desperate situation. In addition, all of the other elements of the defense of necessity were not met. Therefore, **answer C is not the best answer**. In order to be excused for the escape from a prison, the escapee must show that there was no legal alternative, that the harm avoided was severe enough to warrant the violation of a sentence of imprisonment (in most cases, serious bodily injury or death), and that the danger avoided was imminent. In this case, Charlene had been enduring the prison's abhorrent conditions for three years, and could likely have continued living under such conditions for several more years. While the conditions were despicable, Charlene apparently faced no immediate danger. Charlene would not be excused for escaping from the prison because the harm was not imminent and was not sufficiently serious; therefore, **answer D is not the best answer**.

[F] Prevention of Crime

132. **Answer B is the best answer.** In *Tennessee v. Garner*, 471 U.S. 1 (1985), the Supreme Court held that an officer may only use deadly force when she has "probable cause to believe that the suspect poses a threat of serious physical harm, either to the officer or to others." Because Carl was fleeing and did not appear armed, and because the officer had no reason to think that Carl had committed or would commit "a crime involving the infliction or threatened infliction of serious physical harm," the officer was not entitled under the law to use deadly force. Therefore, the officer may not rely upon the defense of crime prevention or law enforcement for the use of deadly force.

Under the common law, police officers had a great deal more discretion to use deadly force to stop crimes or effectuate arrests. However, in *Garner*, the Court imposed a constitutional limit on the police power to use deadly force. Under this precedent, a police officer may use deadly force to effectuate an arrest of a fleeing felon only if the officer has probable cause to believe that the suspect poses a threat of serious bodily harm to the officers or others. **Answer A is not the best answer** because it is too broad and fails to consider the nature of the threat that Carl posed.

The assessment of the risk the suspect poses must be based on the specific situation and the apparent dangerousness of the felon, not broad statutory categories listing "forcible felonies," "inherently dangerous felonies," or "violent felonies." **Answer C is not correct** because it predicates the use of deadly force on the commission of a serious crime rather than on the danger Carl created for the officer or others. *Garner* prohibits an officer from using deadly force unless the felon poses an apparent danger of serious bodily harm either to the officer or to innocent bystanders. Therefore, **answer D is wrong**; the officer may not use deadly force in the prevention of crime or to prevent a felon from escaping when the suspect posed no apparent danger of serious bodily harm.

133. **Answer D is the best answer.** Reasonable force may be used to prevent the commission of crimes. *United States v. Brodhead*, 714 F. Supp. 593, 598 (D. Mass. 1989). Darryl could rely upon the defense of crime prevention for the use of force so long as he reasonably believed that the women were about to commit a crime and that the use of force was necessary to prevent that crime. **Answer A is not correct**. The standard is reasonable force. Tackling a robbery suspect would not seem extreme under the circumstances. **Answer B is also not correct**. Officers may use force either to prevent a crime or to make an arrest. The officer's belief that the force was necessary and that the crime was being (or had been) committed must be reasonable. Moderate force may be used even when there is no danger of bodily harm in order to prevent the commission of a crime. **Answer C is not the best answer** because at the time he used such force to prevent a crime Darryl did not need to fear for his personal safety.

[G] Entrapment

134. Under the majority test for entrapment, the prosecution must prove beyond a reasonable doubt that the defendant was disposed to commit the crime before an agent first contacted her. *United States v. Jacobson*, 503 U.S. 540 (1992). In spite of Cynthia's earlier conviction, it is clear from her reluctance and the several meetings that she was not inclined to sell drugs when Leon first approached her. **Answer D is the best answer**.

Answer A is incorrect, for if the defendant was predisposed to commit the crime, in most states the defense of entrapment will fail even if the agent provided the drugs. While Cynthia ultimately committed the crime willingly, under the subjective test the important moment for consideration is the time before the first government contact is made, so **Answer B is incorrect**. Under the subjective test, the chief inquiry concerns the defendant's state of mind rather than the nature of the government's inducement, thus **Answer C is incorrect**.

135. The objective test for entrapment asks whether a reasonable person would have been induced by the government's behavior to commit the crime. Cynthia may have been more inclined to deal drugs than the average person, but she initially refused to participate in the activities Leon proposed. Cynthia remained hesitant even when faced with dire financial need. She only agreed to deal drugs after Leon had worked very hard to persuade her. Because a reasonable person in Cynthia's position might have been induced to sell drugs based upon Leon's extreme behavior, **answer C is the best answer**. *People v. Barraza*, 591 P.2d 947 (Cal. 1979).

Answer A is not the best answer because Cynthia's eventual agreement to participate in Leon's plan is not relevant to the objective test of entrapment, which focuses on the inducement by the government. The objective test of entrapment examines whether a reasonable person would have agreed to participate in the crime because of the government's actions. The subjective test adopted in a majority of states, see above, examines a defendant's predisposition to commit the crime. **Answer B is not the correct answer** under the objective test because it fails to take into consideration the government's actions, while focusing on the defendant's state of mind. **Answer D is also incorrect**. Cynthia dealt drugs before Leon propositioned her. However, she had quit and had indicated to Leon that she did not want to get back into the business. These facts could be taken into account to determine whether Cynthia was predisposed to commit the crime. While such a determination would be relevant in evaluating a claim of entrapment under the subjective test, it would not be important in evaluating the same claim under the objective test.

136. **Answer D is the best answer.** The subjective test for entrapment looks primarily to the defendant's predisposition to commit a crime rather than the behavior of the government agent. Although the argument could be made that Renée was likely to commit this crime based upon her prior criminal history, her prostitution offenses occurred years before. Renée appeared to have no intention of continuing to engage in prostitution. In evaluating the entrapment defense under the subjective test, courts consider whether the defendant would have engaged in the criminal act absent government intervention. *Sherman v. United States*, 356 U.S. 369 (1958). In this case, it is highly unlikely that Renée would have become involved in prostitution at that time absent the undercover policeman's solicitation for such a large amount of money. Therefore, **answer A is not the best answer**.

Although Renée was willing to commit the crime of prostitution in order to make a large amount of money, the decision-maker using the subject test must examine whether she was otherwise predisposed, prior to being contacted, to engage in prostitution under the subjective test. Therefore, **answer B is not the best answer**. The subjective test considers the culpability of the defendant, whereas the objective test focuses on the government's behavior. The amount of money offered by the police officer would be the crucial factor in an objective test analysis; under the subjective test, however, while the money is relevant, the key question remains: was the defendant predisposed to commit the crime? *United States v. Cerrato-Reyes*, 176 F.3d 1253 (10th Cir. 1999). Therefore, **answer C is not the best answer.**

137. **Answer A is the best answer.** Under the subjective test for entrapment, the important inquiry is whether the defendant was predisposed to commit the crime. In answering this question, the fact-finder can consider evidence of the defendants' prior crimes in order to show their predisposition to commit the crimes charged. The length of time that has passed since the prior crimes, the type of crimes committed previously, and the willingness of the defendants to commit the current crime are all factors that can be weighed in determining the defendants' states of mind. In this case, the students were drug dealers at the time of Fernando's request and quickly agreed to his proposal. For this reason, the government will be able to prove under the subjective test that they were not entrapped by Fernando.

Under either the objective or the subjective test, a defendant can only be entrapped by a government agent, there is no defense of "private entrapment." Nonetheless, the courts have defined the phrase "government agent" broadly to include citizens working for the government. *Sherman v. United States*, 356 U.S. 369 (1958). Because Fernando was acting on behalf of the government, he would be considered a government agent. Thus, **answer B is not the best answer**. Although the police provided the marijuana the defendants sold, the subjective test focuses mainly on the culpability of the defendants, not the actions of the government. The students were exactly the type of people that the police were trying to catch—known drug dealers. The fact that the police provided the drugs is less important under the subjective test than the predisposition of the students to commit the crime; therefore, **answer C is not the best answer**. *United States v. Russell*, 411 U.S. 423 (1973). **Answer D is the wrong answer**. Presumably, no person would commit a crime knowing that she would be caught. The fact that the students would not have sold the drugs had they been aware that Fernando was working for the police does not provide a ground for claiming entrapment. The students cannot show a lack of predisposition to sell drugs simply because they would not have done it in this instance if they had suspected that they would be caught.

138. **Answer B is the best answer.** The objective test allows people who have committed crimes to go free, even if they are culpable. The threat that culpable people may be released provides an incentive for the police to be careful about the methods used to catch criminals. The objective test assumes that even a law-abiding person can be induced to commit a crime if the reward is great enough. The aim of the objective test is to prevent the police from offering such a great incentive for citizens to commit crimes. The subjective test potentially creates different results for the same government behavior based on the defendant's history. For example, the subjective test could preclude a person with a criminal disposition from using the entrapment defense, while allowing a person who had not committed previous crimes to rely on the defense. This result could occur even if both defendants committed the same crime in response to the same acts of a government agent. The objective test addresses this discrepancy by eliminating the evaluation of the individual defendant.

Answer A is not the best answer because it supports the subjective test. The subjective test specifically evaluates the individual defendant's culpability; the objective test explicitly disregards the individual defendant. The objective test may result in the acquittal of guilty people as a cost of preventing police excesses. A basic premise of the objective test is that even reasonable people can be induced to commit crimes. The objective test examines whether an average person would have committed the crime as a result of the government's actions. The subjective test, however, is premised upon the idea that only a person who was already predisposed to commit a crime would be induced to do so. **Answer C is not the best answer** because it supports the subjective test, not the objective test. Law enforcement officials argue that many techniques are necessary to detect certain types of criminal activity. Crimes occurring between consenting, private parties are particularly difficult to discover. Use of undercover police officers and informants may be vital for law enforcement officials to be able to effectively catch criminals, particularly in the drug trade. Although law enforcement officers need a great deal of latitude to be able to effectively perform their jobs, the objective test attempts to create guidelines restricting their behavior. Therefore, **answer D is not the best answer**.

139. **Answer D is the best answer.** Although prior criminal acts are not normally admissible against a defendant to prove a propensity to commit a crime, they may be used to counter a defense of entrapment under the majority, subjective test. When offered for that purpose, the evidence is not used to show a propensity; rather, the prior acts are given to show a defendant's predisposition, or willingness, to commit a crime.

Although answer A may seem to be the best answer, because it is the only choice that does not relate to Wayne's criminal record, **answer A is not the best answer**. As the government may introduce evidence of prior crimes in order to show a predisposition to commit a crime, the evidence in answers B and C would also be admissible. Wayne's drug possession conviction would be admissible, even though it is not the same crime as the one with which he is currently charged. The courts allow a wide range of evidence to be introduced to show that a person was predisposed to commit a crime. The possession conviction and the current charge of selling marijuana are both drug charges, and the possession conviction is recent. Thus, a court would likely allow the previous conviction to be admitted to show Wayne's predisposition to sell drugs. Because the evidence listed in answers A and C would both be admissible, **answer B is not the best answer**. Even though Wayne's conviction for selling drugs was three years ago, the courts take a broad view of evidence that may be used to show a predisposition to commit a crime. Wayne's prior willingness to sell drugs may show that he was inclined to do so again. Once admitted into evidence, the jury must determine whether the defendant was led by the government action or whether he was already willing to commit the crime. **Answer C is not the best answer** because the evidence in answers A and B would also be admissible.

140. **Answer A is the best answer.** The defense of entrapment is never allowed in connection with a serious, violent crime.

Rosaline could not be charged with murder since the crime was not completed; however, she can be properly convicted of attempted murder. Because Rosaline is barred from using the defense due to the nature of the violent crime committed, **answer B is not the best answer**. Police encouragement of murder, particularly in allowing it to progress to the stage that it did with Rosaline, exceeds the bounds of what society expects from law enforcement. However, under both tests, the courts assume law-abiding citizens will not attempt murder and thus cannot raise the entrapment defense. Thus, **answer C is not the best answer**. Regardless of whether the test looks to the defendant's predisposition, or focuses on the behavior of law enforcement officials, as a matter of law the entrapment defense cannot be successfully raised in connection with a charge of attempted murder. Whether or not Rosaline would have committed the criminal act absent police encouragement is legally irrelevant. **Answer D is the wrong answer**.

141.   **Answer D is the best answer.** Courts consider a variety of factors in determining whether the entrapment defense is available to third parties. In this case, Noah's continued participation in the drug lab was vital to the operation. Without Noah, there would have been no drugs and no need for Farah to assist with the distribution. Because Farah would not have become involved in Duane's business without Noah's inducement, she would likely be able to rely on the entrapment defense.

    Answer A is not the best answer. Although Duane was not acting on behalf of the government, Noah was. Duane used the lab's successful operations to induce Farah to work there in connection with Noah. The success of the lab was the direct result of Noah's participation. It would be unreasonable to deny Farah the entrapment defense simply because she was directly approached by Duane instead of his "partner" Noah. Though Farah was willing to participate, that is not the important question. Under the subjective test, courts ask whether the defendant was predisposed. Under the objective test, a determination must be made whether the government inducement was so extreme as to risk criminal actions by the reasonable citizen. Therefore, **answer B is not the best answer. Answer C is not correct**. Courts do not automatically extend the entrapment defense to all defendants; the defense is "defendant specific." Courts consider whether the particular individual was entrapped looking either to her state of mind, or the inducement as to her.

142.   Entrapment law, under the majority test, uses a subjective analysis that primarily considers the predisposition of the defendant to commit the crime charged. In this case, Louis had a reputation as a smuggler and boasted that he could smuggle anything into the country. The government can introduce evidence to show that Louis was willing and able to smuggle the antiques into the country. From that evidence, the jury could find, beyond a reasonable doubt, that Louis was predisposed to smuggle, prior to the officer's request. On this basis, Louis could not raise a successful entrapment defense in most jurisdictions.

143.   The objective test focuses on the behavior of the government. Even if Louis was predisposed to commit the crime, he could be acquitted using the entrapment defense if the government's behavior was sufficiently extreme as to likely cause crimes by a reasonable person. *Bradley v. Duncan*, 315 F.3d 1091 (9th Cir. 2002). In this case, the government official only placed an order on one occasion after

one request. No money was even exchanged. The idea that the government was encouraging illegal smuggling may be disturbing. However, it would be difficult to prove that Louis was already a smuggler without hiring him to smuggle something into the country. Moreover, such actions would not induce a reasonable person to engage in illegal smuggling. Thus, Louis' entrapment claim will likely fail under the minority, objective test.

Entrapment is a defense based upon policy considerations. Therefore, the trier of fact must consider whether the government's behavior should be excused in order to facilitate the conviction of a man who engages in a troubling trade. Here, Louis is unlikely to successfully offer a defense of entrapment under either test.

[H]   Intoxication

144.   **The best answer is answer B.** Although *voluntary* intoxication cannot serve generally as an affirmative defense, one may use evidence of such intoxication to negate one of the elements of the crime charged. *State v. Coker*, 412 N.W.2d 589 (Iowa 1987). As a matter of public policy, most jurisdictions have decided that it would be improper to allow a complete defense of voluntary intoxication because such a defense would permit a drunken person to legally commit acts that he would be held criminally responsible for if sober. Nonetheless, the criminal law is based on individual culpability for actions and allows a defendant's intoxication to be considered to the extent that he had impaired judgment. On this ground, most jurisdictions allow evidence of intoxication to be admitted to demonstrate that a defendant did not exhibit the crime's requisite state of mind. A defendant may escape liability because the prosecution is unable to prove the necessary mental state for the crime, but not because intoxication provides a general defense to the criminal charge. Thus, **answer A is incorrect** in the majority of jurisdictions. As explained above, the defendant would not be prohibited from introducing his intoxication to negate a state of mind requirement. However, in a small number of jurisdictions, intoxication cannot be introduced as evidence for any reason in connection with any charge. The constitutional challenge to this rule was rejected by the Supreme Court in *Montana v. Egelhoff*, 518 U.S. 37 (1996).

   Answer D is incorrect because it looks to the government's failure to prove an element of the charge, rather than as an affirmative defense, which is what the question asked. **Answer C,** which suggests that a constitutional limit may be present in this case, **is incorrect**. While the Supreme Court has held that laws that punish drug addicts (and possibly alcoholics) merely for their status as addicts violate the Constitution, these individuals can still be criminally sanctioned for the acts that they commit. *Robinson v. California*, 370 U.S. 660 (1962). For example, an addict in possession of illegal drugs can be convicted of possessing illegal substances, even though she could not be convicted merely because the state demonstrates that she is a drug addict and, therefore, must be in possession of drugs at all times.

145.   Although evidence of intoxication could not be used as a general defense to the crime, Mark could escape liability if his intoxication precluded the prosecution from establishing one or more of the requirements for the charged crime. Evidence of

intoxication could allow the defense attorney to create a reasonable doubt that Mark had the requisite state of mind to commit the charged crime. Reckless behavior can establish the state of mind requirement for various homicide offenses, however, so the fact that Mark became inebriated would not defeat the prosecution. The finder of fact could well conclude that he acted in a grossly reckless fashion, thereby causing the death. Given this possibility, and the availability of lesser charges such as involuntary manslaughter, it seems unlikely that Mark would escape criminal liability altogether.

146. **Answer C is correct.** In most states, evidence of intoxication is allowed to negate the mental state element of the crime, particularly if it is a high state of mind, classified at common law as specific intent. Inchoate offenses, such as attempted murder, are specific intent crimes. Thus, **answer D is wrong**.

Answer A is incorrect because it instructs the jury as if the defendant's intoxication, in and of itself, is a defense. **Answer B is not the best answer** because in no state is voluntary intoxication classified as a true defense. Rather, evidence of voluntary intoxication may be relevant to show that the defendant did not possess the necessary state of mind.

147. **Answer A is the best answer** because Brandi involuntarily consumed a strong drug that caused her to lose control and kill. Involuntary intoxication operates as a true defense. *Torres v. State*, 585 S.W.2d 746 (Tex. 1979).

Answer B is not the best answer, because while Brandi chose to drink punch, she did not choose to consume an illicit drug, one that she could have known had a chance of leading to unusual behavior. Contrary to answer C" involuntary intoxication can present a defense in a prosecution for a person who takes a substance without knowledge or reason to know that it was intoxicating in nature. Involuntary intoxication could also be a defense if a person was forced to take an intoxicating substance against his or her will. Thus, **answer C is incorrect. Answer D is incorrect** because Brandi may rely on the defense of voluntary intoxication if she drank voluntarily, but without knowledge of the substance in the punch.

148. Yes, for the defense of voluntary intoxication is based upon the view that if an individual is wholly without fault in consuming the affecting substance, she ought not to be held criminally responsible. Where she has been forewarned, even if she did not fully believe the warning, it would have been utterly irresponsible of her to go ahead and drink a large amount of the suspect beverage. In such a situation, the intoxication would not likely be seen as involuntary, so the defense would fail.

[I] The Insanity Defense

149. **The best answer is answer B.** This response correctly identifies the so-called *M'Naughten* test, followed in a majority of jurisdictions. *State v. Savoie*, 349 N.W.2d 139 (Mich. 1984). The test, also known as the "right/wrong test," demands that the defendant, at the time of the crime, not know the difference between right and wrong because of his mental condition. One of the main criticisms of the *M'Naughten*

test is that it does not accurately encompass different kinds of mental illnesses. The test focuses exclusively on mental illnesses resulting in cognitive failures. For example, the test does not consider a mentally ill person who understood that killing someone is wrong, even though she was unable to conform her behavior to that knowledge. Such criticism led to the adoption of a new test, the "irresistible impulse" test used in answer C. This test, used in a minority of jurisdictions, also has its critics, for it focuses exclusively on control and avoids issues concerning cognition or awareness. Therefore, **answer C is incorrect.**

Answer A is incorrect in that it invokes the so-called "product test," also known as the *Durham* rule. *Durham v. United States*, 214 F.2d 862 (D.C. Cir. 1954). This test requires that the jury determine whether the disease *caused* the crime, a determination even mental health professionals usually cannot make with certainty. Few states retain this test. **Answer D is also incorrect** in that it sets out the Model Penal Code's approach to the insanity defense. This test allows for a person not to be held responsible for an action, even if he knows the action is wrong, if he does not "appreciate" the moral significance of the act. *State v. Johnson*, 399 A.2d 469 (R.I. 1979). This rule combines both the right/wrong analysis and the irresistible impulse rule. In these ways, the Model Penal Code approach is thought to give the jury the greatest role to determine the culpability of the defendant, which helps to reduce the problem of expert witnesses usurping the role of the jury in determining culpability.

150. Yes. Under the right/wrong formulation of *M'Naughten*, the judge need only admit evidence that relates to the one specific question, namely whether the defendant knew that his actions were right or wrong. If, as stated above, Jeff understood the killing was wrong and knew that it was illegal, then the evidence of his justification could be excluded as irrelevant. *Commonwealth v. Bruno*, 407 A.2d 413 (Pa. 1979).

151. **The correct answer is answer A.** Expert testimony in insanity defense cases can be extremely helpful. Typically, however, experts are precluded from testifying to the ultimate question of insanity; that issue is for the trier of fact. *United States v. Brawner*, 471 F.2d 969 (D.C. Cir. 1972). Testimony by an expert as to whether Jeff suffered from a mental disease and whether that disease caused the killing is clearly outside the scope of proper examination of a witness. It would be highly unlikely that a judge would allow such testimony from an expert. Thus, **answer D is wrong**.

Answer B is incorrect, as the *M'Naughten* rule actually requires that the killing be undertaken because of the mental defect. As such, the determination as to whether Jeff's mental illness caused him to kill it is of vital importance. An expert's testimony in this regard would be excluded, but not because it is irrelevant. **Answer C is also incorrect**. As noted above, while the jury must determine if the defendant meets the insanity standard, conclusory expert testimony is excluded because the jurors must make those determinations themselves.

152. **True.** Unlike other affirmative defenses such as self-defense, where some states put the burden on the defendant and others require the state to disprove the defense,

the burden of proof as to insanity lies with the defendant in most jurisdictions. Typically, the state must prove the defendant's guilt beyond a reasonable doubt. At that point, the burden shifts to the defendant to demonstrate the requirements of the insanity defense, usually by a preponderance of the evidence. In the federal system, however, the defendant must prove the insanity defense by clear and convincing evidence, an even higher standard. 18 U.S.C. § 17. Legislatures have imposed particularly stringent requirements on those seeking to invoke the insanity defense for a variety of reasons, largely because of the widespread belief that the insanity defense may be too easily achieved. In fact, the insanity defense is seldom invoked and rarely succeeds.

153.   **Answer C is correct.** Most states do not allow a judge to raise the insanity defense over the objections of the defense, even if a judge feels that such an instruction is appropriate. Unless the defendant is not competent to make the decision, the determination is to be made by him and his lawyer. *United States v. Marble*, 940 F.2d 1543 (D.C. Cir. 1991). **Answers A and B are not the best choices** because they reflect the older approach to this problem. Traditionally, the judge was either obligated to instruct on the defense, or at least allowed to do so, if she saw evidence that might convince a reasonable person that the defendant met the requirements for the insanity defense. **Answer D is incorrect**, as the basis of the law here is not the probability of the success of the defense. Rather, the focus here is on which person has the right to make that decision.

[J] Diminished Capacity

154.   **Answer C is the best answer.** Evidence of mental illness can be used to defeat the government's showing of state of mind, often referred to as diminished capacity. *State v. Smith*, 396 A.2d 126 (Vt. 1978). In contrast to the insanity defense, which asserts that the defendant committed the crime but should not be held responsible because of mental illness, a claim of diminished capacity states that the defendant could not be found guilty of the crime because she lacked the mental ability to form the requisite state of mind (*e.g.*, intent or premeditation). Here, if the jury finds that Deborah was mentally incapable of premeditation, it cannot find her guilty of first-degree murder. This would be true even if Deborah does not meet the jurisdiction's insanity requirements. Therefore, **answers B and D are incorrect**. Such evidence is relevant to the government's charge of murder. The first-degree murder charge would fail for lack of proof if the defendant did not have the required state of mind, regardless of whether or not the insanity defense was raised.

Answer A is incorrect because evidence from friends and family may be sufficient to cast doubt on a defendant's state of mind. The defendant at trial is allowed to paint a full picture of her mental state, particularly if lay testimony is supplemented-as here-by expert-testimony. *Commonwealth v. Larkins*, 489 A.2d 837 (Pa. 1985).

155.   No special instruction on the evidence is required in this instance. If the jury finds beyond a reasonable doubt that the government has shown all of the elements of the crime, including the mental state requirement, Deborah will be convicted. Because the insanity defense is not being raised and is not available for the jury's

consideration, no special consideration need be given to the evidence of her mental illness in this case. Just as there would not need to be any special instruction concerning misidentification or alibi, no special instruction is necessary here. A judge may hesitate in delivering a special instruction on this evidence as it might give such evidence undue influence over evidence of equal merit (*e.g.*, an alibi or physical evidence) tending to cast doubt upon the government's case. However, the judge would have the discretion as to whether to offer a jury instruction on this issue. If she feels that there is some confusion on this difficult issue, she may instruct the jury on the above information. *State v. Jackson*, 714 P.2d 1368 (Kan. 1986).

[K] Competency to Stand Trial

156. **The best answer is answer D.** The issue of competency to stand trial arises when the defendant's current mental capacity is in question. This can be distinguished from the insanity defense and diminished capacity, both of which focus on the defendant's state at the time of the crime. A defendant may be found incompetent to stand trial if she cannot understand the nature of the proceedings against her or if she cannot consult with her lawyer with a reasonable degree of rational understanding. *Dusky v. United States*, 362 U.S. 402 (1960). Competency and insanity are not exclusive of one another. That is, a person who was legally insane at the time of the crime may also be considered incompetent at the time of trial, but the court's evaluations of each issue remain distinct. With the evidence involved here—Danilo's deteriorating mental state—competency should be raised in order to gain consideration of this evidence before trial.

Answer C is incorrect because the competency matter must be resolved before trial, before any other substantive legal questions can be answered, and because this evidence goes more to a competency issue than to an insanity defense. For this same reason, **answers A and B are incorrect**. This evidence should not be delayed until trial, to be used in evaluating Danilo's guilt or innocence. If he is declared competent to stand trial, the evidence may then be relevant as to several points. First, though, competency must be determined.

157. **The best answer is B.** If the government is able to prove that Angie intended to kill her boyfriend, she most likely would be convicted of voluntary manslaughter. This crime involves a killing "in the heat of passion," where the perpetrator intends to kill the victim, but only out of some extreme emotional exchange of some kind, such as a violent argument. The rule is that the exchange must be a legally adequate provocation. *People v. Wharton*, 809 P.2d 290 (Cal. 1991). While words alone would not generally be enough to constitute a legally adequate provocation, words plus the slap might be sufficient. **Answer A is incorrect** because Angie does not seem to have acted with premeditation.

If the government demonstrates that Angie intended to kill her boyfriend, a conviction for negligent homicide is not the probable outcome. This charge requires only a negligence standard, not intent, and usually applies to accidental killings. Thus, **answer C is not the best answer. Answer D is incorrect** because intoxication provides no true defense under the law. Evidence of intoxication can be used to raise a doubt as to whether the defendant was able to form the requisite intention to commit a crime. On these facts, however, the government has proven intent, so Angie's intoxication will be of no assistance to her case.

158. **The best answer is A.** The only evidence that suggests that Tom intended the crime be committed is that he took Bart to the station and did not object. This evidence could just as easily lead to the conclusion that Tom only wanted to get away from the actual criminal as soon as possible. Tom was in a dangerous situation and likely feared for his life. Under such circumstances, there would be insufficient evidence of an agreement, the essence of the crime of conspiracy. *People v. Mariano*, 934 P.2d 315 (N.M. 1997). Thus, **answer D is incorrect**.

Answer B refers to the defense of withdrawal, which is not available in all jurisdictions. If Tom is otherwise found to have been a conspirator, a claim that he had withdrawn from the conspiracy, if even accepted in his state, would fail. The jurisdictions that allow withdrawal as a defense would also require that Tom communicate his withdrawal to Bart and to try to prevent the crime. For example, Tom would have had to report the robbery to the police immediately. Therefore, **answer B is incorrect. Answer C is incorrect as well.** While it details Tom's involvement in the crime, the key finding for a conspiracy conviction is that there was an agreement to carry out the crime. Such an agreement is not present here.

159. **Yes**, because it would make a finding of agreement much more likely. If Tom was aware that Bart was a criminal, it would make his decision to pick him up less innocent looking. Any attempt by Tom to claim that he acted only under duress would seem much less credible, because Tom intentionally placed himself in a dangerous situation. In addition, the fact that they know each other and had a shared history

of committing these sorts of crimes is much more strongly suggestive of an agreement. The finding of an agreement would only be inferred from all of the circumstances, but if a jury finds that there was an agreement in the actions of Tom and Bart, either explicit or implicit, Tom would be found guilty of the conspiracy charge. *Direct Sales Co. v. United States*, 319 U.S. 703 (1943).

160.   **The best answer is A.** Under the felony murder rule, as it exists in most states, liability will extend to any foreseeable death that results from the committed felony and allow for a conviction of felony murder. *People v. Matos*, 634 N.E.2d 157 (N.Y. 1994). The reason for such a conviction is to hold criminals responsible for the consequences of their dangerous actions, even if there are unintended consequences. The rule applies to forcible felonies, like kidnapping, because these crimes are by nature so dangerous that a consequential loss of life is said to be generally foreseeable.

   Answers B and C are incorrect. Whether Matt intended for Tamara to die is not the focus of the felony murder rule. The key inquiries under the felony murder rule are whether any inherently dangerous felony was intended and whether the killing occurred during the commission of that felony. Here, Matt intended to commit kidnapping, he did so, and the woman was killed while he carried out his felonious purpose. **Answer D is also incorrect** because the felony murder rule eliminates inquiry into such intent. Moreover, accidents are foreseeable when transporting victims.

161.   **The best answer is B.** As a co-conspirator, Kim can be held responsible for the foreseeable actions of her co-conspirator. *Pinkerton v. United States*, 328 U.S. 640 (1946). This policy of holding members of a conspiracy accountable for the actions of their partners will lead a jury to find her guilty of murder. Even though the plan was not to use weapons, it is often held that weapons are foreseeable even with a contrary understanding. **Answer A is incorrect** because Kim is only responsible if the death was foreseeable.

   Answer D is wrong. Kim, as a co-conspirator engaged in a kidnapping, will face the same legal consequences as Matt. It is without significance that the killing with a gun by Matt was accidental, because the broad rule as to responsibility applies. Co-conspirators are held for the foreseeable acts that take place. Therefore, **answer C is also incorrect**.

162.   **Answer C is the best answer.** Evidence of a defendant's mental illness can be used in furtherance of an insanity defense. It can also be used in an attempt to negate the intent element of the crime, under the diminished capacity doctrine. *Commonwealth v. Larkins*, 489 A.2d 837 (Pa. 1985). The evidence of Jennifer's condition was therefore relevant to issues at trial. In effect, the defense strategy may have been able to claim that because of her mental illness, she was unable to form the requisite intent to agree to a conspiracy or to rob the bank. Such an approach can be viewed as an assertion that the government has failed to prove all of the necessary elements, a failure of proof claim. Therefore, **answer A is incorrect.** Conspiracy requires proof that the defendant intended to agree to

commit some crime, and as such, the ability of a defendant to form such intention is relevant. Thus, **answer B is wrong**. **Answer D is incorrect** because the evidence as presented does not compel such a finding.

163. **The best answer is A.** Courts today hold that a judge no longer has the ability to raise the insanity defense over the defendant's objection. *Frendak v. United States*, 408 A.2d 364 (D.C. App. 1979). A court must defer to a defendant's decision to waive the insanity defense if a competent defendant made that decision intelligently and voluntarily. Thus, **answer D is wrong**. Competency issues must be raised prior to trial. *Pate v. Robinson*, 383 U.S. 375 (1966). As Jennifer's case was being presented to the jury for a verdict, Jennifer must have already been deemed competent to stand trial. Therefore, **answer B is incorrect**. **Answer C is also incorrect**. Here the defendant contended through the course of trial that she was not guilty and that the government could not prove its case against her. To then have the jury presented with an entirely contradictory instruction from the judge on the insanity defense, which generally presumes guilt as its premise, could certainly be seen as harmful to the defendant's cause.

164. The first question, which asked if the defendant suffered from a mental illness, might be considered acceptable. The second, however, would be impermissible. Concerns about expert testimony are especially pervasive in the context of the insanity defense. The difficulty is that the *jury* must find whether or not the defendant qualifies as insane. Especially in instances of complex technical or professional evidence, juries may give too much weight to the testimony of an expert and, in effect, allow the psychiatric opinion to determine the outcome of the case. For this reason, courts and lawmakers have attempted to exclude from expert testimony anything that speaks to the "ultimate issue." *United States v. Brawner*, 471 F.2d 969 (D.C. Cir. 1972). Clearly the second question is precisely the question that the jury needed to answer, and Dr. Phil should not have been permitted to answer it. The first question, though, is more complicated as it goes directly to the witness' expertise based—presumably—on his professional evaluation of Jennifer. Many courts would allow the expert to answer this question.

165. Shopkeepers do not generally owe any duty of warning to customers in connection with the sale of lawful products. Still, under the homicide offenses of murder (implied malice) or manslaughter (involuntary) any person is prohibited from engaging in reckless behavior that causes death. Walt may not have understood, at the start, what was happening with all the teens buying household cleaning products, but he certainly was made aware of the phenomenon when he spoke with his son. As a result, he could be found to have been consciously aware of the great risk created by the continued sale of these products. By not only selling them, but also increasing his stock in them, he could be found criminally responsible for either involuntary manslaughter, or perhaps even for second degree murder. *Commonwealth v. Feinberg*, 253 A.2d 636 (Pa. 1969).

166. **The best answer is A.** Betty was in a unique position to help Martin, being employed by him. As such, she was under a duty to come immediately to his assistance. Thus, she could be found guilty of manslaughter or even murder. *Commonwealth v.*

Pestinikas, 617 A.2d 1339 (Pa. 1992). While a charge of negligent homicide would be one possible outcome of Betty's case, the facts could allow a jury to determine that Betty was more than merely negligent. Therefore, **answer B is not the best answer. Answer C is correct**, but only in the abstract. Although a duty to come to someone's assistance is generally not imposed in the criminal laws of this country, there are exceptions when the person is in a unique position to prevent harm to another. As Martin's nurse, Betty held such a position and could be found to be contractually and criminally responsible for his welfare. Such callous disregard for her patient's condition might indeed lead to a charge and conviction for a serious homicide offense. **Answer D is not the best answer** because it suggests that Betty did not cause Martin's death. However, a jury could decide that withholding his medication and failing to provide prompt medical assistance did in fact cause his death.

167. Dirk and Eric would certainly raise a First Amendment challenge to prevent their convictions. Because their speech is politically motivated, they could not be convicted based upon the content of their message. *Commonwealth v. Jones,* 888 S.W.2d 544 (Ky. 1994). The First Amendment's protections would forbid such a prosecution on that basis. Localities can, however, place limitations on the location and volume of the speech. Thus, the First Amendment challenge will likely fall, with the state relying on the manner of the speech, not its content. The statute under which the state proposes to prosecute the two may have Fifth and Fourteenth Amendment Due Process problems. The so-called "void for vagueness" doctrine dictates that laws must be sufficiently clear to put the public on notice. A reasonable person must be able to discern the meaning of the code language. As it stands, it appears that this provision could be determined unconstitutional under the Due Process Clause. The scope of the law seems indeterminate, in particular, the definition of "unreasonable noise." Even if the law holds up under Due Process scrutiny, the defendants could argue that, as applied, the statute is invalid as their speech was not "unreasonable" under the circumstances. The use of the powerful bull horns may discredit that argument. It may also demonstrate that the defendants intended to cause "public inconvenience, annoyance or alarm," as required, and not simply to offer an anti-government message.

168. **Answer A is the best answer.** Under the majority, subjective test for entrapment, Mark's defense would likely succeed. This test, as used by the Supreme Court and a majority of states, looks to the defendant himself to see if he was likely to commit the crime without the influence of the government. Here, Mark was reluctant to take drugs again and vigorously resisted Pedro's efforts. Only after an extended period of inducements did Mark finally succumb. The government may have a difficult time showing beyond a reasonable doubt, as it must, Mark's predisposition to possess drugs. *Sherman v. United States,* 356 U.S. 369 (1958).

Answer B is incorrect, for a Due Process violation can only be based on a truly shocking abuse of governmental power, certainly not present here. **Answer C is incorrect** because an informer is considered an agent of the government if he is closely tied to the investigation. **Answer D is not the best answer** as it suggests something similar to a "but-for" test, which may be a reasonable approach in determining whether entrapment occurred. Similar to a subjective test, such an inquiry would determine culpability dependant on whether the defendant would have engaged in the criminal behavior but for the influence of the government actor. Even under this standard, Mark may be able to show that he would not have returned to drugs had it not been for the overbearing influence of his false friend and government actor.

169. **The correct answer is B.** At common law, the fleeing felon doctrine allowed an officer to shoot a suspect in order to prevent flight from the scene of a felony, if the officer had probable cause to believe the suspect had committed a felony. The Supreme Court, however, has imposed a much stricter standard on law enforcement. *Tennessee v. Garner*, 471 U.S. 1 (1985). Now, for such a justification, the officer must show that the suspect posed a continuing serious danger to others. The commission of a burglary, as in *Garner*, is not enough to demonstrate such danger, for often burglars are unarmed and do not threaten others. Here it appears that the suspect would not have posed any obvious danger to others simply because he was running and was likely a burglar. As such, **answers A and C are not the best answers**.

Answer D is also incorrect. While an officer may only intend to wound a suspect to prevent further flight, criminal liability is imposed if the officer kills the suspect or seriously injures him. In considering whether deadly force was necessary under the circumstances, the court will balance the competing interests at stake and determine that the government's interests in arresting an escaping burglar are outweighed by the individual suspect's interests in life and good health.

170. **The best answer is C.** If a child is alive even for a matter of moments, it is deemed to be a viable human being. Under the traditional definition of homicide—the killing of a human being by a human being—the actions of Adam would constitute murder. *Keeler v. Superior Court*, 470 P.2d 617 (Cal. 1971). **Answer A, therefore, is incorrect**, as no such showing of future life is required.

Answer B is wrong for two reasons. First, as the father of the child, Adam owed a duty of care to the infant. Second, it was not his failure to take care of the child that is the basis of the homicide prosecution; rather it was his affirmative action in suffocating the child that is the subject of the case. **Answer D is also wrong** because the standard rule is that to be a human being for homicide purposes the child must survive the birth process, if only for a short period. While some states have enacted infanticide statutes, or laws that expand the definition of "human being" for homicide purposes, most states have not.

171. **The best answer is D.** A conviction for rape requires the government to prove that the defendant, through force or threat of force, had intercourse with the victim without that person's consent. **Answer A, therefore, is wrong**. However, rape shield laws generally prohibit evidence of prior sexual encounters from being introduced by the defense. *See, e.g.*, Tenn. Code Ann. § 40-2445. One reason for such laws is to prevent the victim's character and sexual history from becoming the focus of the trial. In addition, even if the defendant demonstrates that the victim

has had sex consensually with other partners, it would not necessarily follow that she consented to sex on the occasion in question. Thus, **answer B is wrong**. **Answer C is not the best answer.** Although Answer C may otherwise be correct, as a result of rape shield laws, the defendant will be barred from even offering the evidence. Therefore, the better answer is answer D.

172.   **The best answer is C.** In most jurisdictions, an attempt offense can only be successful if the prosecution shows that the defendant took a substantial step toward the commission of the crime, or a step in close proximity to the crime. *Minshew v. State*, 594 So.2d 703 (Ala. 1991). Stella's steps were very early in the process; she could well have changed her mind before driving to the boss's house and confronting him. Her actions were simply preparation, far short of what would be needed, even if her purpose was certain. **Answer A, then, is incorrect, as is answer B.** It is not the number of steps that determines if an attempt has been taken, but rather how close those steps get toward the commission of an offense. **Answer D, however, is wrong**, as no state requires for the attempt offense the last possible step prior to the completion of the crime, as that would create too many dangers for effectively stopping purposeful criminal actors.

INDEX

INDEX

TOPIC	QUESTION